SPOOKY
Great Lakes

Also in the Spooky Series by S. E. Schlosser and Paul G. Hoffman

SPOOKY
Great Lakes

*Tales of Hauntings, Strange Happenings,
and Other Local Lore*

RETOLD BY S. E. SCHLOSSER

ILLUSTRATIONS BY PAUL G. HOFFMAN

Globe
Pequot
ESSSEX, CONNECTICUT

Globe Pequot

An imprint of Globe Pequot, the trade division of
The Rowman & Littlefield Publishing Group, Inc.
4501 Forbes Blvd., Ste. 200
Lanham, MD 20706
www.rowman.com

Distributed by NATIONAL BOOK NETWORK

Copyright © 2024 by S. E. Schlosser

Illustrations copyright © Paul G. Hoffman

British Library Cataloguing in Publication Information available

Library of Congress Cataloging-in-Publication Data

Names: Schlosser, S. E., author. | Hoffman, Paul G., illustrator.
Title: Spooky Great Lakes : tales of hauntings, strange happenings, and other
  local lore / retold by S. E. Schlosser ; illustrations by Paul G. Hoffman.
Description: Essex, Connecticut : Globe Pequot, [2024] | Series: Spooky
  series | Includes bibliographical references.
Identifiers: LCCN 2024010564 (print) | LCCN 2024010565 (ebook) |
  ISBN 9781493085699 (paperback) | ISBN 9781493085705 (epub)
Subjects: LCSH: Ghosts—Great Lakes (North America) | Haunted places—
  Great Lakes (North America)
Classification: LCC BF1472.U6 S2953 2024 (print) | LCC BF1472.U6
  (ebook) | DDC 133.10977—dc23/eng/20240416
LC record available at https://lccn.loc.gov/2024010564
LC ebook record available at https://lccn.loc.gov/2024010565

∞™ The paper used in this publication meets the minimum requirements of
American National Standard for Information Sciences—Permanence of
Paper for Printed Library Materials, ANSI/NISO Z39.48-1992.

For my family: David, Dena, Tim, Arlene, Hannah,
Seth, Theo, Rory, Emma, Nathan, Ben, Deb, Gabe,
Clare, Jack, Chris, Karen, and Davey.

Welcome to the family, Elora Annabelle Mertz! We love you.

Contents

Contents

Contents

SPOOKY SITES . . .

① Grand Marais, MN

② Apostle Islands, WI

③ Marquette, MI

④ Milwaukee, WI

⑤ Hammond, IN

⑥ Presque Isle County, MI

⑦ Traverse City, MI

⑧ Saginaw, MI

⑨ Detroit, MI

⑩ Toledo, OH

⑪ Put-in-Bay, OH

⑫ Cleveland, OH

⑬ Rochester, NY

⑭ Niagara Falls, ON

⑮ Toronto, ON

⑯ Thunder Bay, ON

⑰ Isle Royale National Park, MI

⑱ Duluth, MN

⑲ Douglas County, WI

⑳ Deer Park, MI

㉑ Sault Ste. Marie, ON

㉒ Door County, WI

㉓ Green Bay, WI

㉔ Chicago, IL

㉕ Grand Haven, MI

㉖ Mackinac Island, MI

㉗ Port Huron, MI

㉘ Erie, PA

㉙ Buffalo, NY

㉚ Kingston, ON

AND WHERE TO FIND THEM

Introduction

Lighthouses have always played an important role in Great Lakes folklore, and many of them have ghost stories attached to them, so I was eager to visit one during my spooky research trip. I headed out early on the second day, enjoying the bright sunshine and cool breeze over Lake Erie. My destination that morning was the haunted Fairport Harbor lighthouse and museum.

When I arrived, I found the building was closed, since it was offseason. But I couldn't be sad when there was a lovely beach on Lake Erie's shore right next door and gorgeous walkable grounds on the property. I spent a happy hour wandering about taking photos and musing on the various haunted lighthouses that populated the whole Great Lakes region. My favorite tale was of a fisherman, caught in a squall on Lake Huron, who was guided to safety by a ghostly beam from a nonfunctioning lighthouse ("The Big One"). The Fairport Harbor lighthouse with its ghost cat was another fun addition to local lighthouse lore, so I kept my eyes peeled in case I encountered the phantom feline while walking about the property.

Next, I headed to the haunted Rider Inn in Painesville for lunch. It was a wonderful atmospheric old inn and tavern from the 1800s. The ghost of Suzanne, the old innkeeper's wife, and the spirit of a Civil War soldier were said to haunt the property. While I ate a chicken salad wrap for lunch, I pondered the story of the Red Rover, whose captain returned after death to save his crew when the ship sprang a leak on its way to Toledo. And there was another tale about the War of 1812 Memorial in Put-in-Bay. It was said to be haunted by the spirits of those who perished in the Battle of Lake Erie.

After lunch, I headed to another lakeside park, where I discovered that the retaining wall was made of huge boulders filled with fossils. I had a great time climbing around the rocks and looking at imprints from the far past. While I sat peacefully watching the wind ruffle the tops of the waves, my mind wandered to Cleveland, one of the next stops on my spooky travels. An almost-forgotten tale spoke of a farmer walking home one autumn night who had a vision of his uncle dying in a snowstorm, which was sadly confirmed by letter several weeks later ("Sudden Snow"). Another Great Lakes prophecy was given to a surfman working at a life station on Lake Superior's shipwreck coast. The surfman dreamed of a well-dressed man begging for help during a terrible storm. He later found the man's body while doing a sweep of the beach. The man was identified as the captain of the *Western Reserve*, a steamer that cracked open from the pressure of a storm just 35 miles northeast of Deer Point. His family and most of his crew perished while trying to make it to safety after the ship went down ("The Dream").

My last stop of the day was to the Thomas Edison birthplace, where I met a peacock named Percy gracing a tree by the parking lot and then purchased a ticket to tour the house next door. When I was upstairs in the bedroom, I got chills looking into the exhibit showing Edison's cloak and shoes. Was the ghost of Thomas Edison still here? It seemed possible.

After saying goodbye to the ladies in the museum (and Percy), I headed back to the hotel for the evening. My Spooky Great Lakes tour was off to a good start.

Happy Hauntings!
Sandy Schlosser

PART ONE
Ghost Stories

1

Retired Captain

GRAND MARAIS, MINNESOTA

Corsair was a retired sea captain who settled on a farm outside Grand Marais in the spring of 1890. There were all sorts of rumors about his prior career. The gray-haired, swarthy man with the scarred face and robust manner seemed more suited to the life of a buccaneer than a backwoods farmer. His house was filled with curious objects from around the globe: cutlasses, conch shells, exotic fans, spices, and ivory carvings. Town gossip labeled him a pirate hiding out from the law, and nothing I saw of the man contradicted this theory.

Corsair liked to hang out at the tavern in the evenings. I met him several times when I dropped in for a drink before dinner. Over time we became friends, and the wife and I would have the old man over to our place for a meal now and then. Corsair liked talking about the amazing places he'd been before taking up farming. Since I'd traveled myself before and after attending law school, I appreciated hearing his stories, even though I strongly suspected the old salt of editing the tales to make himself sound on the up-and-up.

I once asked Corsair how he ended up in Grand Marais. He replied: "My grandfather was a voyageur who passed through these parts trading furs back in the day. He thought it was the most beautiful place in the world. He wanted to move the family here, but Grand-mère wouldn't allow it. When it came time for me to . . . retire . . . I remembered Grand-père's stories and decided to fulfill his lifelong wish."

One evening, Corsair showed up at my law office just as I was preparing to close for the day. A beautifully carved wooden box was cradled in his arms. "Thought you and your missus might appreciate this. Got it off a ship . . . um, ah . . . I *found* it in a marketplace on a Far East voyage back when I was a first mate. I always thought it should belong to a lady," he added, opening the lid to show me a porcelain tea set. I protested the expense of such a gift, but he wouldn't take no for an answer. He thrust it into my arms and hurried away before I could thank him.

Corsair must have had a premonition of his own mortality. A month after his visit to my law office, he was found dead in his bed. The doctor said he died of natural causes. In his will he asked my law office to administer his estate. I ordered the house locked until potential heirs could be found to claim it.

A few nights afterward, the missus and I were awakened by a brute of an autumn snowstorm, the first of the season, that slammed into the house and shook the rafters. It was so loud that we had trouble sleeping, and I prayed to heaven that no one was out and about in this dreadful weather. The next morning I cleared walkways to the house and barn and then tramped through thigh-deep snow to the neighbor's house to check on Madame Laurent and her boy, since her husband was away visit his ailing mother. I found the boy struggling to get to the barn, so I helped him clear snow and tend their livestock.

Then we settled into the kitchen with Madame Laurent to thaw out and discuss what else needed doing while her husband was out of town.

Just then, the man himself walked into the house, red-cheeked and out of breath from tromping through such thick snow. "Had to leave the horse at the livery in town and hoof it home," Laurent told his wife after their first greetings were over. "The snow is head-height in some places from all the windfalls."

"Where did you stay the night?" asked his wife. "I was afraid you might be caught outside in this terrible storm!"

"I almost was," Laurent said cheerfully. "But I reached Corsair's house just before the snow started and figured it would be safer to bunk in with him than try to fight my way through the huge storm massing on the horizon. I put my horse in the barn and knocked on the back door of the house. I thought I saw a light moving around inside, but no one answered the door. I figured Corsair wouldn't want me to freeze to death on his doorstep, so I forced the door and built a fire in the kitchen to ward off the chill." He shivered, remembering the cold. "I lay down by the fire to rest and fell asleep at once. I only came awake when old Corsair stepped into the room. I apologized for entering without his permission, but he didn't seem to hear me. I think he was sleepwalking. He wandered around the room as if searching for something, then left without saying a word. I heard him walking around most of the night, during pauses in the storm."

I shook my head in disbelief. "You must have been dreaming," I said briskly. "Old Corsair died a week ago and is buried in the church graveyard."

Laurent stared blankly at me. "Dead? That's impossible. I saw him last night."

"We went to his funeral, Papa," said the boy solemnly. He was 12 and a bit of a hellion, but truthful for all his wild ways. Laurent believed him.

"Well I'll be . . . " He sank down onto a kitchen chair as if his knees had suddenly failed him.

"It must have been his ghost," Madame Laurent said. She was the practical member of the family. "So why is his ghost still haunting the house?" She looked at me questioningly.

"You are assuming it wasn't a dream," I pointed out. "That's a big assumption. Laurent was tired after a long day of travel and very cold from the approaching storm. That's enough to make anyone dream."

"I'd swear it was real," Laurent said suddenly. His face was still pale, but his eyes were determined. "If old Corsair's spirit is haunting the house, we should find out why and ask it to leave."

I didn't believe in ghosts, but I could see the matter would disturb my friend and his family until it was resolved.

"There's only one way to be sure," I said. "We will go there tonight, after you've had a rest, and investigate."

Around eight o'clock that night, Laurent, his son, and I tied our horses to the fence post at the edge of the road and tramped our way through snowdrifts toward Corsair's house. As we approached, a low moan filled the air. I stopped abruptly, goose bumps rising all over my body.

"What was that?" gasped young Laurent, clutching his father's sleeve. We heard someone curse, and then the sound of a sword being drawn from a scabbard emanated from the empty house. Lights appeared, first at one window, then another.

RETIRED CAPTAIN

"Thieves," I yelled suddenly, recovering my aplomb. "They're stealing from the estate!" I pulled out my gun and fought my way through the snow to the door. Laurent and his boy followed. I unlocked the door and we burst inside, ready to fight. But the inside of the house was dark and cold and still.

I fumbled to light the candle we'd brought with us. Its light revealed an empty, dust-covered room. The curios from Corsair's former life were as still as I'd last seen them when I'd locked up, and there were no dusty footprints on the floor. I moved through the house rapidly, followed by Laurent, looking in each of the rooms. Most were undisturbed, and the only changes in the kitchen were the forced door, the ashes in the fireplace, and the clean spot where Laurent had slept on the hearth. The back door had reopened an inch or two, but when we looked outside in the flickering candlelight, the only footprints were Laurent's.

As we gazed perplexed around the empty kitchen, a wild wind swept through the house, blowing dust everywhere and extinguishing our solitary candle. A ghostly voice swore aloud, and something fell with a massive thud that shook the whole house. We stared at one another, shaking in our boots. Laurent's eyes widened. "Where's my son?" he gasped and ran from the room. I followed, heart thundering with fear. We traced the noise to one of the front rooms. As I entered, I saw that a board had been wrenched out of the wall, and behind it was a hollow that made the perfect hiding place. Then I saw the boy lying on the floor. He had a big lump on his head as if someone had clubbed him with a stick, and his hands were clenched around a bag full of coins, some of which had spilled around his fallen body.

Laurent dropped on his knees, calling the boy's name in alarm. "Son, wake up!" he cried, slapping the boy's face, shaking his shoulders.

Suddenly, an angry shout reverberated through the room. My hair stood on end, and Laurent whirled to look at the empty hole in the wall. The glowing figure of Captain Corsair, cutlass in hand, stood before the desecrated hiding place.

"Corsair put a curse on his money," I gasped in sudden understanding.

The ghost strode forward, swept the bag of coins from the limp boy's hands, and thrust them into the secret hiding place. Then he vanished with a bang, and the wall was whole once more.

We carried the injured boy home, where the doctor patched up his head and told us he was lucky to be alive. While Laurent consoled himself with a bottle of whisky, I commissioned the local carpenter to board up the haunted house while my office searched for any legal heirs.

The next evening, I went to the inn where I first met Corsair and told the town gossips that I had confiscated the bag of coins and sealed it away in a bank vault until the rightful heirs had been found. When they asked if I'd had trouble with the ghost, I told them Corsair had appointed me as his estate manager, so his ghost had not interfered when I took the coins from their hiding place. This story was a falsehood. I had not returned to the haunted house, nor did I intend to do so. But I felt it was necessary to spread the rumor in order to keep treasure hunters away from the property. I did not need any more ghost-inflicted injuries, or, heaven forbid, a death, on my conscience. It was apparent that only the rightful heir of the deceased would have any possibility of surviving in the haunted house while the vengeful ghost stood guard over his money.

When no one came forward to claim the property after a year of searching, I had the haunted house burned to the ground, money and all. I wasn't taking any chances on another person coming to grief. Let the ashes return to the soil. Maybe then, Corsair's curse would wear itself out.

2

Frozen Dawn

APOSTLE ISLANDS, WISCONSIN

It was like our honeymoon all over again. The kids were in college now, and both of them had decided to work during the summer months, which left me and the wife free to tool about the Great Lakes in our Bermuda-rigged sloop for the whole month of August. We were headed for the Apostle Islands—probably our favorite vacation spot in the entire world—and we made good time that trip. Pulled into dock at the marina in Washburn, brought out our camping gear and our sea kayaks, and prepared to roam any and all of the 22 islands that were part of the park.

Our aim that first day was for Long Island, a small gem off the southern tip of Madeline Island. Located on the northwest tip of the Chequamegon Point barrier spit, it was shaped like a half-moon with sandy beaches on the shoreline and forest in the center. Home to two lighthouses and the remains of a third, Long Island was surrounded by shallow water that prevented cruise boats from coming too close. Anyone wishing to camp on the island made their way by water taxi or private boats. That was fine by us. We liked the privacy of the island and always camped there the first night we arrived in the Apostle Islands

National Lakeshore. It was a great spot for bird-watching, being one of the nesting grounds for the endangered piping plover.

We turned in early after a sunset stroll along the beach. I slept deeply and would have been content to sleep the whole day through, but my wife woke me just before dawn, wanting to kayak around the island as the sun rose and the world awakened. The light was still dim, and there was no sound anywhere—no birds, no wind whispering in the trees, no rustle of nocturnal animals hurrying to their homes. The hush was so complete that it felt eerie. Neither my wife nor I was inclined to talk as we silently launched the sea kayaks and began softly paddling around the island toward the LaPointe lighthouse. The lake itself was like glass, barely lapping at the strangely silent shore. To me, the soft splashing noise made by our paddles was a desecration in that waiting silence.

As we drew near the spot where the ruins of the 1858 lighthouse lay hidden by the trees, a cold chill swept through the air, ruffling the water around the kayaks and making me sneeze. My wetsuit did nothing to alleviate the terrible chill, and for a moment, I thought I saw snowflakes in the crystal-clear air around us. Then my wife gasped aloud and pointed. I tore my eyes from the snow and followed her gaze.

To our left was a wrecked barque laying in about 17 feet of water with her bow pointing to the east. Her rigging stretched like skeletal hands up out of the depths, the only piece of her visible above the water. Lashed to the masts—one in the main and two in the mizzen—were the bodies of three dead sailors, covered with ice. One figure was heavily dressed, but his feet were bare and his heavy mustache was hard to discern beneath the ice that crusted it. Another had a sandy beard and heavy clothes with high-topped boots. The third was just a small man, quite young, with light clothing unsuitable for the terrible cold and high-topped boots. The look on their frozen faces would haunt my dreams for many months to come.

"Dear God in Heaven," my wife whispered, her words producing a white cloud in the frigid air. We stared at the wreck in fear and awe as the grayness of dawn was slowly replaced by color. The first rays of the bright summer sun came over the horizon, piercing the grisly scene so that it shimmered and then faded away.

Warmth returned to the world with the disappearance of the ghostly vision, breaking the uncanny hush that had filled the predawn hour. Suddenly, the wind was dancing across the water of the lake, stirring and rippling it softly around the kayaks, and birds were singing and scolding and flapping around on the shore of the island.

"Were we dreaming?" my wife asked shakily, paddling back a foot or so in her nervousness. Wordless, I pointed to the front of my kayak, where ice was slowly melting away in the heat of the summer sun.

"There . . . there are snowflakes in your hair," my wife whispered. I reached up and touched one, and it melted on my fingers.

"I'm going back to the campsite," my wife said abruptly, expertly turning the kayak and hustling through the waters at top speed. I had a hard time keeping up with her.

We beached the kayaks and walked back to the tent together.

"Honey, what was that?" she whispered, huddling close to me. I put my arm around her, as much to comfort myself as to comfort her.

FROZEN DAWN

"I think we caught a glimpse of the shipwreck of the *Lucerne*," I told her solemnly.

The *Lucerne* was a schooner barge that had grounded just off Long Island in a November gale in 1886. She arrived in Ashland in tow to the steamer *Raleigh*. The *Lucerne* was loaded up with 1,256 tons of iron ore consigned to Luttle, Ogleby & Co. of Cleveland. She set out to rejoin her tow steamer in Sault Ste. Marie, Ontario, but charged headfirst into a nor'easter instead. Caught in heavy snow squalls and gale-force winds, the *Lucerne* turned and tried to reach the safety of Chequamegon Bay. She was in view of the LaPointe lighthouse when she wrecked, and all of her crew was lost. Several men were swept overboard, and three of the sailors—those we had seen—had lashed themselves to the masts in an attempt to save themselves from the frigid waters of Lake Superior. It hadn't worked.

Both the lighthouse keeper and early morning fishing boats discovered the wreck, and rescue boats arrived in the early afternoon to remove the bodies from the rigging and take them to Ashland for identification. The stern of the ship was found a half mile east of the lighthouse with the words "Lucerne, Cleveland" painted on her arch board. The body of the mate washed ashore soon afterward, but the other crew members were never found.

My wife sat on the ground in front of our tent, hugging her knees with both arms as she listened to the tale of the wreck. "Those poor, poor men," she whispered, wiping a tear from her cheek. I nodded soberly, remembering their faces underneath the ice. We sat silently for a long time, listening to the awakening island and thinking our own thoughts. Then my wife rose to her feet and said: "I think I'd like to leave the island right now, Honey. I hope you understand."

And I did. I too wished to leave behind this haunted place. We packed up our belongings, stowed them in the kayaks, and paddled northward toward Madeline Island. Neither of us looked back.

We didn't report our strange adventure to anyone in the park. Who would believe it? Even now, I have a hard time reconciling myself to the memory. If my wife hadn't seen it too, I would have dismissed the whole thing as a dream. But we both saw it, plain as day, and the memory is etched inside me for all time. I'm not sure if I will ever return to Long Island again. Maybe. But if I do, I won't go kayaking at daybreak. I'll leave those predawn hours to the ghosts.

3

The Merchant

The sailor had hightailed it out of Bay City on the first ship he could find—which was an old schooner barge called the *Comrade*. He left behind an unfaithful wife and her lover, both rather the worse for wear after he discovered them together and tossed the lovestruck man out of their bedroom window—their second-floor bedroom window, that is.

The sailor thought it best to make himself scarce before his wife could complain to the police, so he hurried down to the docks to look for a ship. The *Comrade* was in tow to a steamer called the *Columbia*, and neither ship was in good shape. But the sailor figured anything was better than jail, and so he joined the crew, taking watches and doing his duty while keeping his head down and staying quiet.

The trip north to Ashland went without a hitch, and they were heading back toward Cleveland, steaming past the Keweenaw Peninsula, when a heck of a large southwester came roaring out of Lake Superior, churning up the water and blowing everything to kingdom come. Massive waves the size of houses buffeted both ships, and it wasn't long before the hawser tying them together came loose and the *Comrade* was set adrift.

There was no way the *Columbia* could retrieve the schooner barge in that mighty storm, and her captain wasn't fool enough to try.

The sailor had been on the lakes since he was a lad of 10, but never had he seen such a storm. Without the *Columbia* to help them, he figured they were all doomed. He was just glad he'd had the opportunity to throw his wife's lover out the window before he went to meet his Maker.

The barge rolled from one side to the other in the thrashing waves. It sank lower and lower, until suddenly it fell out from under the sailor's feet and he found himself fighting for his life beneath the water, kicking and struggling against the massive undertow caused by the sinking ship and swimming for the only marginally lighter water near the surface. His head broke through at last, and he gasped for breath, treading water and trying to see in the midnight-darkness of the storm.

The sailor was in the trough of a giant wave when he emerged from the depths, and it wasn't until he reached the next peak that he saw the yawl only a few yards from him. He struck out immediately for the small sailboat, the only thing left from the *Comrade*, and dragged himself aboard. The sails were tattered to bits, and the sailor didn't even try to steer. He just hung on for dear life as the storm bellowed and raged around his shivering, soaking-wet body.

He was lucky it was summertime, or he would have died of exposure and cold before the storm rumbled away. The tumult was followed by an eerie calm, and a thick fog worthy of merry old England. The sailor shivered and snuffled and rubbed his arms to keep out the cold, wondering where the yawl was taking him. Suddenly, a huge black shadow loomed through the fog, and he heard a voice: "Ahoy there, the yawl! Do you need help?"

The sailor blinked in bewilderment, roused himself from his stupor, and shouted a reply. Within a few moments, he found himself being hauled up onto a big, old-fashioned, top-masted schooner, and his yawl taken in tow behind the ship. In a daze, he was shuffled kindly into the fo'c'sle and given clean, dry clothes. The cook brought him a thick, rich stew that heated up his insides and made him drowsy. He was asleep before he lay down in the bunk they made up for him, and he didn't wake until late the next day.

The sailor was welcomed gladly by captain, crew, and passengers. He soon learned that he was on a schooner called the *Merchant*, bound for Eagle Harbor on the Keweenaw Peninsula. The ship was carrying a load of mining equipment; strange cargo to the sailor's mind, since the Keweenaw hadn't been actively mined for many years. Several of the passengers claimed to be miners, and their rough clothing and hearty manner seemed to substantiate their claim. There were also a few lumberjacks on board, and one soldier. The sailor thought it odd to find a soldier aboard the ship in these peaceful times, but he was in no mood to worry. He was too busy feeling grateful to be alive.

The passengers took turns talking to the sailor, demanding details about the shipwreck and particulars about his home. One old fellow wanted to know what year it was and who was president. This question baffled the sailor, and he began to wonder why the passengers seemed so disconnected to the present.

THE MERCHANT

Overhead, the sky was blue, and the wind whistled cleanly through the air, filling the sails of the *Merchant*. They were making very good time. As the sailor relaxed, ate, and chatted with the passengers, the ship sailed on and on and on, moving ceaselessly toward the wide horizon.

It was around noon on the third day that it finally dawned on the sailor that something was wrong. It should have taken them no more than a day, by his reckoning, to reach port. So why were they still sailing? The ship was traveling the right direction and seemed to be moving briskly. But no land was in sight. And no one else seemed to have noticed their lack of progress.

Uneasy, the sailor started watching the crew and passengers as he made his way around the ship. He noted, as he had when he first arrived onboard, that their speech was old-fashioned, and their clothing out of date. Now it dawned on the sailor that—aside from the day they pulled him aboard—he had never heard the passengers discussing the world outside the ship, or what they intended to do when they disembarked. They acted as if they never expected to leave the *Merchant*, as if the ship were their whole world.

That night, the sailor woke from a terrible nightmare. In his dream, he was chained up in the darkest hold of the ship, never more to see the light of day. He had faded away there, until he was nothing but a ghostly voice calling for the crew to let him out. As the sailor bolt upright in bed, shaking with fear, he suddenly remembered a story an ancient mariner had once told him about a schooner called the *Merchant* which left the Soo one clear day in 1847. The ship was bound for Keweenaw Peninsula and was carrying supplies for the mines that were still active at that time. But the ship never made her destination, and she was presumed lost somewhere on Lake Superior.

The sailor shivered, realizing only then that he was sheltering aboard a ghost ship, doomed to sail on forever, never reaching her destination. He wondered if he himself were dead. He thought not; but he might as well be, he decided, if he stayed aboard the *Merchant*.

The sailor slipped silently from his bunk, careful not to disturb the sleeping passengers who shared his room, and crept cautiously up on deck. Avoiding the night watch, he made his way down to his yawl, released it from its mooring, and slipped inside. As soon as he was free of the wake of the schooner, he began rowing for shore with all his strength, guiding himself by the stars. After an hour, the wind blew up from the north and sent the yawl careening toward the distant land. The water became so choppy that the sailor could do nothing but hang on and hope for the best. Toward dawn, he saw the coastline appear on the horizon. And a few hours later, the yawl capsized in the surf at the shoreline, and the sailor dragged himself onto the beach.

After resting, the sailor hiked inland until he found railroad tracks. He followed them until he was overtaken by a lumber train. He hitched a ride on the last car, and soon the train rolled into Marquette. Realizing that he still had his wallet, the sailor walked into the local tavern, ordered food and drink, and struck up a conversation with a captain taking shore leave. Working the conversation around to local events, the sailor learned to his horror that the *Comrade* had been lost—presumably with all of its hands—in a storm three months previous. What had seemed to the sailor a three-day journey on the ghost ship had actually taken three months! It would not have taken long for him to die of old age at that rate.

Thankful to have escaped, the sailor secured a berth on the captain's ship under an assumed name, remembering just in time that he was a wanted man in Bay City. Since he was presumed dead, the sailor figured he'd better stay dead for the duration, rather than risk a jail cell down the road.

The sailor never saw the ghost ship again, though he often thought about the poor *Merchant* and her crew, doomed to sail forever toward the Keweenaw Peninsula without ever reaching their destination.

4

The Shrouded Horseman

When the Civil War ended, Jeremiah Jones, once a slave, found himself a free man. Eager to make a new life for himself, he made his way north to Milwaukee. For several years, he worked odd jobs as a dockworker, loading and unloading the ships that brought their wares to sell in the city. He finally earned enough money to buy himself a big white horse and a dray—a low, flatbed wagon without sides. Shortly thereafter, he was hired on as a drayman with the Phillip Best Brewing Company.

Jeremiah would begin each day by stopping his dray wagon in front of the stone-lined hillside vaults that resembled caverns, where the beer kegs were chilled. Once his wagon was loaded, he would begin his delivery rounds, greeting everyone with a cheerful smile and a joke that delighted the brewery's customers and earned him a good reputation among the Best management staff. He was so industrious and trustworthy that he was given more responsibilities and better pay. Jones quickly earned enough to buy property on the outskirts of town. He built a beautiful little cottage and a big barn for his white horse and dray.

Once he was settled into a home of his own, Jeremiah decided it was time to marry. He had his eye on a pretty girl named Lucille whom he had met while out on his deliveries. Whenever duties permitted, he'd park his dray near Lucille's house, and the two lovebirds would laugh and talk together. Sometimes they'd walk shyly along the road, and he'd give her wildflowers he'd brought from his cottage garden.

No one in Lucille's family considered the relationship more than a casual friendship, so they were taken completely aback the day that Lucille came home and announced that she and Jeremiah had just been married by the justice of the peace. Her parents were surprised by the match but quickly resigned themselves to the situation, not wishing to alienate their only daughter. But for Lucille's brother James, it was entirely another matter. He thought that Lucille had married beneath her station, and he hated the former slave for stealing his sister's heart. James was so enraged that the drayman had presumed to marry his only sister that he turned bright red and couldn't speak for a full five minutes after Lucille broke the news. Then he grabbed Jeremiah by the collar and kicked him roughly out of the house, using the most offensive language imaginable. Jeremiah did not dignify the foul words with a response, but Lucille, watching, knew that he would not soon forget his treatment by his new brother-in-law.

James followed Lucille up to her room and begged her to have the marriage annulled. Ignoring him, she calmly packed her bags—tossing them out of the window to her new husband when James blocked the door—and then climbed out of the same window and down the wisteria vines to the grass below.

Lucille left her parents' home forever in the dray drawn by the large white horse, and she never set foot in that part of the city again. She and Jeremiah lived simply but happily in their little cottage by the woods. Lucille's mother sometimes stopped by to visit and would spend the day sewing with her daughter and chattering about their friends and neighbors. Nothing was ever said about James, who had loudly disowned Lucille the day she married Jeremiah and left home.

Three months had thus passed when Lucille returned home from a Ladies' Aid Society meeting early one evening to find an empty house. This was strange because Jeremiah was usually done with the chores by that time and could be found sitting at the fireside intently reading the daily newspaper. She glanced around the small cottage, puzzled by his absence. Grabbing up a lantern, she went out to the barn.

As Lucille approached the wide double doors, her heart started pounding. There was an oddly metallic smell in the air— the smell of blood. Something was wrong! Lucille wrenched the barn doors open and stepped inside. The light of the lantern fell onto a bloodstained floor. Then she saw the broken body of her husband lying a few feet away. With a scream, Lucille ran to him and knelt down in a puddle of blood.

"Jeremiah," she cried. "Jeremiah!" There was no response. She hadn't really expected one. There was so much blood all over the floor. No one could have lost so much and still be alive.

Time had slowed down for Lucille. Each second ticked by like an age as she placed the lantern with exaggerated care on the floor beside her husband's body, reached out with shaking hands, and turned him over. His face was battered almost beyond recognition; his arms and legs broken in several places.

Half-hidden under his leg she saw a familiar silver pocket watch—one that she had last seen attached to her brother's waistcoat.

"Oh, Jeremiah," Lucille sobbed, pulling his bloodied body into her arms and rocking back and forth in agony. "Oh, my love."

Her screams had alerted their neighbors, Charlie and Jane, who came running to find out what was wrong. Charlie took one look at the mess inside the barn and immediately sent Jane home. He tried to get Lucille to get up and go with her, but she didn't even seem to notice he was there. She just kept sobbing as she clutched Jeremiah's body in her arms.

It was a long time before Charlie could persuade Lucille to lay the body down. He helped her to her feet, and she watched dully as her neighbor covered Jeremiah with a thick horse blanket. Then he escorted her firmly back to the cottage and asked Jane to minister to the stricken woman.

Walking back to the barn, Charlie went to check on the white horse and was not surprised to find it lying dead with its throat cut. A few feet further on, Jeremiah's dray lay smashed to pieces. Charlie shut the barn doors carefully on the scene and went to summon the sheriff.

Lucille's brother had fled the city by the time the sheriff arrived at his house to question him regarding Jeremiah Jones's murder. A warrant for his arrest was put out, but James was nowhere to be found. After the funeral, Lucille put the cottage up for sale and went to live with an aunt in Madison, unable to bear the thought of staying in the city where she had lost her husband. No one in the area wanted to buy the house, thinking it had been tainted by such a brutal murder, so it remained

THE SHROUDED HORSEMAN

empty. Charlie and his wife looked after it for Lucille whenever they had time to spare. And that was that. Everyone thought this story had ended, and life in Milwaukee went on as usual. Until one evening at dusk, when the phantom appeared.

It was Charlie who first saw the ghost. As he rode his horse into the barnyard early one evening, the animal suddenly reared with a terrified whinny and Charlie was almost thrown. He wrestled for control and finally managed to bring the horse back down on all fours. Only then did he look up and see the dray drawn by a glowing white horse coming slowly down the road. It was driven by a tall figure wearing a gray shroud that whipped and flapped under the force of an invisible gale. The wheels of the dray were a good two feet above the surface of the road. It took all of Charlie's strength to keep his terrified horse from bolting as the phantom drayman turned down the lane toward the Jones place and passed out of sight. Charlie had recognized the horse and dray at once. The spirit of Jeremiah Jones had returned a month to the day after he had been killed.

Sightings of the ghost became frequent in that section of Milwaukee. It was not uncommon for fellows to stagger into the local tavern, white as a sheet, and collapse at the bar for a few drinks after seeing the shrouded figure driving toward them with its robes flapping in the unearthly wind. There was something menacing about the phantom, which drove all the highways and byways, as if it were seeking something or someone. Charlie was convinced that Jones had returned to avenge himself on his murderer and would not rest until he found him.

About six months after the sightings began, Charlie was summoned to his front door one evening at dusk by a harsh knocking. His wife looked up in alarm, and Charlie motioned for her to stay in the kitchen as he went to open the door. Standing on the porch was a drunken, red-faced figure that he recognized at once as Lucille's brother, James.

"Where's Lucy?" the man slurred, looming over Charlie until their noses almost touched. "I looked for her on the farm, but she ain't there. Where's she?"

"Lucille has gone away," Charlie said, motioning to his wife behind him with one hand. Go get the sheriff, he willed mentally to her. Go get the sheriff. He heard the back door click softly and knew she was on her way. Now all he had to do was keep James occupied until the sheriff arrived.

"We've been taking care of the cottage for her," he said, trying not to breathe in the alcoholic fumes that were wafting off the tall, swaying figure. "Would you like to see it?"

"My cottage now," slurred the elder brother. "I earned it!" He chuckled to himself, obviously delighted by the crime he had committed against his sister and her husband.

Charlie led him off the porch and walked slowly across the farmyard to give his wife time to run down the road to the sheriff's place, which was half a mile away. Lucille's brother wasn't in good shape for walking, anyway. He staggered this way and that, first bumping into the fence and then tripping over the front gate. As Charlie stepped out into the road, a cool breeze unrolled over the landscape like a frozen carpet. Charlie gasped, his eyes fixed on a point of blue light down the road.

"Whatcha stopping for?" grumbled James, righting himself and giving the gate a vicious kick for good measure. Charlie didn't answer. He couldn't speak. Always before, when he'd seen the phantom, it had been calmly driving along in its dray. But tonight, the dray was careening down the road with the shrouded figure standing up in its seat, cracking his long whip ferociously. The white horse was wild-eyed with fury. It picked up speed when it saw the man who had killed it and its master, and it gave a scream of anger that turned Lucille's brother around in his tracks.

With great presence of mind—considering the circumstances—Charlie stepped back behind his fence, leaving Lucille's brother to face the music alone. The drunken man stared at the glowing figures pounding toward him down the road. He swayed left. He swayed right. He stumbled backward, trying to find his feet. On the fourth try, he managed to sort out his left leg from his right and fled with a scream that was all the more terrified for its delay in coming to his throat. He scuttled down the road, weaving back and forth, with the drayman and his horse thundering at his heels, the horse snapping at his back and the glowing whip cracking across his shoulders. Charlie watched them until they disappeared out of sight.

A few minutes later, Jane came racing home, her blue eyes huge with amazement and fear. "Did you see?" she gasped. "Did you see?"

"I saw Jeremiah chasing that no-good brother of Lucille's down the road," Charlie said.

Jane nodded vigorously. "The phantom got him just as the sheriff and I came out his front door. The ghost snapped the end of the whip around his leg and pulled him off his feet. Then the horse and dray drove right through him! James gave a sort of gasp and then flopped onto the ground, dead as a mackerel, with a look of sheer terror on his face. And serves him right too," she added. "Nasty, horrible man. Justifiable homicide by a ghost, the sheriff called it. I'm going inside right away to write and tell Lucy."

She marched into the house, and Charlie followed her, after sending one more incredulous glance down the road to the place the phantom had appeared. He had a feeling that this was the last time they would ever see the ghost of Jeremiah Jones—and he was right.

5

Sophia

HAMMOND, INDIANA

The taxi driver was startled when a woman in white waved him down as he was driving into Hammond. Still, a fare was a fare. As he pulled up, he realized her fancy gown was, in fact, a wedding dress. The style was old-fashioned, but it looked good on her. She was young, with long blond hair and stunning blue eyes. She must be a model on her way to a photo shoot, the taxi driver thought admiringly. He couldn't think of any other reason a lovely lady in a wedding gown should be hailing a taxi.

As the woman stepped into the back, the air in the taxi cooled abruptly, as if the driver has turned on the air-conditioning—which he hadn't. The man shivered a little as he glanced in the rearview mirror and asked the lovely bridal figure for the address. She told him to drive to Cline Avenue in Hammond. The driver nodded and pulled out into traffic.

"You doing a photo shoot?" he asked, unable to control his curiosity.

At first the woman did not answer. The taxi driver glanced into the rearview mirror, afraid he'd offended her with his question. When he saw her ashen face and trembling lips, he stuttered an apology. But the woman shook her head.

"No apology," she whispered. "The fault is not yours. It is mine. I thought . . . I thought . . ."

Her voice broke on the last word, and she lifted a dainty hand and wiped her eyes. The taxi driver tore his attention away reluctantly and kept his eye on the road as she told her story.

She was seeing a man from the other side of town against her parents' wishes. They wanted her to marry a man from their own nationality, and her boyfriend came from another part of the world entirely. Still, the couple loved one another in spite of their differences, and they met often on the banks of the Calumet River. They planned to wed secretly, and she had saved all her money and bought the perfect wedding gown. Then she snuck away after work one day to meet her boyfriend at a local church where a priest had agreed to marry them. She'd dressed herself carefully in the new wedding gown and had waited and waited and waited for her groom to arrive. But he never came. After two hours, the priest had gently urged her to return home, and she had reluctantly agreed.

"Oh miss, I'm so sorry," the taxi driver began, glancing in sympathy at the white-gowned woman pictured in the rearview mirror. Then he gasped. The woman in the back seat no longer wore a pristine white wedding gown. Now she was soaked to the skin, her white wedding dress torn and covered in mud and river slime. Her face and her lips were blue, and she didn't seem to be breathing.

A desperately honking horn brought his attention back to the road. He'd swerved into the next lane while his attention was on the woman in the back, nearly causing an accident. The driver fought for control of the taxi and managed to get over to the side of the road just before the bridge over the Calumet

SOPHIA

River. He threw the taxi in park, put on his hazard lights, and whirled around to face the woman in the rear. The back seat was empty, except for a damp patch on the seat and the smell of river water in the air.

The taxi driver clutched at his heart in shock. What? How? He fell back against the seat and took long slow breaths, trying to calm himself. Then he put on his blinker and pulled back into traffic, wondering what the heck had just happened to him.

He thought about the eerie incident all the rest of the day. Finally, he told one of his buddies about the incident. His buddy had been driving a taxi in Hammond for a long time and didn't seem surprised by the story. He said: "Did she ask you to take her to Cline?"

"How'd you know?" the taxi driver asked in astonishment.

"That was Sophia," his buddy said. "She's been haunting that stretch of highway for a long time. She didn't tell you the end of her story. The day her boyfriend left her waiting at the church, she ran outside and hailed a cab to take her home. But when she reached the stretch of Cline Ave near the bridge, she told the taxi driver to halt. Then she leapt out of the cab, raced frantically down to the edge of the water, and threw herself into the river before the cabdriver could stop her. She was swept away by the current, and her heavy skirts pulled her under the water. She drowned, and the fishermen found her body a few days later, floating along the shore in her ruined wedding gown."

The taxi driver shook his head in sorrow, remembering the tears the woman in white had shed in his back seat.

"Poor girl," he murmured. "Poor abandoned girl."

"They say her fiancé was killed in a mill accident the day before the wedding. That's why he didn't show," his buddy said.

"Did anyone ever tell Sophia that?" asked the taxi driver. "Maybe it would help her to rest in peace."

"You do that, the next time she asks you for a ride," his buddy said, half in jest.

"Maybe I will," said the taxi driver. But remembering the drowned figure in his back seat, he wasn't so sure he wanted to give Sophia another ride in his taxi. Once was enough.

6

The Big One

They warned me. All of them did. Huron is finicky. It was the wrong time of year to stray far from shore. Squalls come up suddenly. Temperatures can drop to freezing all at once. Waves bouncing off land from all sides can swamp the boat. It was not like boating in Florida. *Blah, blah blah.*

All I could think about was the trophy fish on my cousin's wall. In all my years of fishing, I had never caught one that size. Must. Have. Fish.

My fishing boat in Florida was set up with every imaginable gadget under the sun. My cousin's was bare bones in comparison. How had he caught that fish?

Against everyone's wishes, I went out on Lake Huron that afternoon with every conceivable form of rod and bait I could fit into the fishing boat. My cousin offered to come with me, but nope. Just nope. I could barely be civil to him after I saw that fish. Sure, he knew the Great Lakes better than me, but I knew fishing boats. How hard could it be?

The lake was choppy when I set out, but nothing I couldn't handle. The sun was out and the water that gorgeous Huron blue. What a lovely day. The warnings of my family seemed unwarranted at best, sour grapes at worst. My cousin knew I was the better fisherman.

I was several miles from shore when the big one hit. Boy howdy, it took my line and ran. I had never heard of whales in the Great Lakes, but it felt like I'd hooked one. Run, dive deep, circle, come up, run again. The tussle between us was fast and furious. Sweat was running down my face, and the chilly breeze that rose up around the boat as we fought for supremacy felt good. It was glorious. And when I finally landed the monster fish after more than an hour, I was almost crying with delight. Me! The tough guy. Crying over a fish. But he was the biggest darn fish I'd ever caught. Bigger than the one on my cousin's wall.

My arms were so tired, I almost couldn't get him over the sides of the boat in the eerie green light that had crept over the scene while we fought. The boat was shuddering and twitching in the rough chop. I'd thought it was because the fish was pulling it about so hard. But now that the big one was aboard, I realized it was because another monster was nearly upon me. A monster storm.

I was shaking with fatigue, but I got a jolt of adrenaline when I saw those roiling clouds bearing down on me with fire in their midst. The whole world was a greenish mist already darkening toward night, and the waves already were almost the size of the boat. That's when I remembered all the warnings. When storm surge hit the lakeshore, it bounced back from all sides, making the waves even more deadly than a typical surge.

I swallowed hard and looked around, trying to get my bearings. Where had the dad-blamed shore gone? Had the monster fish really dragged me so far? I consulted my compass, got my boat turned in the right direction, and grimly tried to outrun the storm.

Thirty minutes later I was soaked to the bone and shivering from cold. There was sleet mixed with the rain, and my light windbreaker wasn't helping. Every other wave slapped more water on me and the boat and the monster fish in the bottom. I was fighting to keep the boat upright and heading in the general direction of home, but the waves were every bit as bad as everyone said, and I was numb from cold and exhaustion. *Fool, fool, fool,* I cursed myself. I would be lucky to make it home alive at this rate. A couple times, I thought I'd be struck by lightning, and more than once a rogue wave almost turned me over. Worse, the cold was making my brain foggy, so my reflexes weren't so good.

Darkness had descended with the storm, and I couldn't make out any shore through the thick sheets of rain. I was pretty sure I was a dead man piloting, but I kept going toward what I hoped was shore.

Suddenly, an amber-colored light flashed across my vision. I startled upright. I hadn't realized I'd slouched down so low over the wheel. I'd been losing track of what I was doing until the flash came. The Coast Guard, I thought, relief washing over me. But I didn't see the shape of a cutter anywhere nearby, and there were no running lights visible through the heavy downpour.

The light came again, sharp and bright. Once. Again. Again.

It was a lighthouse. An older lighthouse, I presumed, based on the color and pattern of the beams. Probably an old-style Fresnel light. Glory be, I was saved.

THE BIG ONE

I aimed for it, through the stinging sleet, the flashes of lightning, and the freezing wind, waves slopping water almost continuously into my boat, which sank lower and lower as I fought the elements to get to land.

It was almost pitch black when the waves tossed the boat up onto a small stretch of shore that wasn't quite a beach. I pulled the floating swimming pool that was once my cousin's fishing boat as high up as I could manage in my benumbed state and tied it off so the waves wouldn't drag it away.

I'm not quite sure if the events that happened next were real, or if I was in some kind of exhausted dream state. I remember tying up the boat and staggering through the heavy sleet and rain toward the whitish tower topped with the glowing light. *Warm. Must get warm.* It would be ironic if I died from hypothermia after thwarting those terrible waves.

Suddenly, a man appeared before me. He was surrounded by a glowing light, and it took my exhausted brain a heartbeat to understand the brightness pouring through an open doorway. It's the lighthouse keeper, I thought, fatigue sweeping over me suddenly as I realized I was rescued. I heard him exclaim over my bedraggled state and felt strong arms catch me as I fell. And then everything went black.

I woke in front of the flickering flames of a fireplace. I was wrapped in a blanket, warm and almost dry. The old keeper's worn face appeared above me. He was clean-shaven except for a voluminous white goatee on his chin, and his kind eyes were creased with concern. He gave me a glass of water to drink, and a moment later I fell asleep.

The next thing I recall was a hand shaking me awake and a voice in my ear saying, "Storm's over, son, and the waves have died down enough to be navigable. Your wife is worrying. Time to go home."

I nodded vigorously. My wife would be frantic by now. I thanked the kind man and staggered outside to a lovely day with no trace left of the storm, save a slight breeze and the choppy surface of Lake Huron.

I untied the rope with hands that shook only a little. The boat was a little worse for wear, like me, but it was large enough to handle the post-storm surf. And the Big One was still on ice and would make it home just fine.

The day was warming up quickly, and the ice from the storm was already gone as I pushed away from shore. I checked my compass, started up the motor, and turned the boat in the direction of my cousin's home.

I followed the shoreline for several hours before I started recognizing landmarks. That storm had really knocked me off course. My wife and cousin were shouting and crying as I pulled into the dock with my wild tale and my prize-winning fish.

"We've had the Coast Guard out looking for you," my wife sobbed in my arms. "I thought you were dead!"

"I pulled ashore by an old lighthouse, and its keeper took me in until the surf died down," I told her, hugging her back.

My cousin gave me a funny look. "An old lighthouse?" he asked. "Where exactly were you?"

I shrugged. "No idea. A little peninsula with an old lighthouse and a keeper's cottage. Real old-fashioned place. It felt like I stepped back in time."

I got goose bumps as I said it. It was true. It felt like I'd slipped through a crack in time last night. I wasn't sure how much of what I remembered was an exhausted dream and what parts were real. The only certainty was that I'd seen a bright beam of light from the old lighthouse just when I was sure I was a goner, and it led me to safety. It was only now that I was back home that I realized just how strange the night had been. And that man, the lighthouse keeper, he'd been blazing with light when I first saw him. Like an angel. Or a ghost.

My knees gave out and I dropped onto the dock. My wife shouted in alarm, and everyone simultaneously tried to lift me up and carry me into the house, which totally didn't work. I got my feet under me and waved them off. "Get my fish," I snapped at my cousin. "And someone call the Coast Guard and have them stand down. I'm fine."

My cousin jogged off dutifully to obey these tasks, while my wife led me indoors so I could have a hot shower and a rest.

The rest of our vacation was uneventful. Just the way I wanted. I'd had enough adventures, at least for a while. My cousin and I had my fish weighed, mounted, and delivered to my house in Florida, where it was given pride of place on the living room wall.

A few months later, I was flipping through a book on Great Lakes lighthouses when I saw a picture of the lighthouse that had saved me from the squall. According to the text, it had been decommissioned many years ago and was no longer operative. So my hunch was correct. I'd been rescued by a ghost.

It sounded too crazy to believe, so the only one I told was my wife. She just smiled and said, "See? My prayers brought you home."

Remembering the lighthouse keeper's parting words, I knew she was right.

The Seagull

TRAVERSE CITY, MICHIGAN

The men in our family have been Great Lakes sailors for generations. Members of our family like to say that we have lake water running in our veins instead of blood. My great-great-granddaddy started out as a commercial fisherman, and each generation followed in his footsteps until my father broke with tradition and became a "salty," traveling across the Great Lakes, through the Saint Lawrence River, and out to sea. I took a job on one of the "lakers"—a Lakes bulk freighter—as soon as I got enough schooling, and worked my way up to captain as fast as I could.

My home port was Detroit in those days, though I did not see my home or my wife nearly as much as I would have liked. But she never complained—she was a true captain's wife. We had one child, a boy, who inherited the family love of the water. He was a better sailor than I by the time he was 10, and my wife and I were very proud when he joined the Coast Guard.

I had married late and was getting on in years by the time our boy was grown. I'd squirreled away enough money to retire early. It was not long after Charlie started his career on the Lakes that I ended mine, much to the quiet relief of my wife.

I'd survived one too many lake hurricanes, and we both knew I was lucky to have lived to old age.

During the early spring, the wife and I packed up our things and moved north to Traverse City. We still had access to a commercial deep-water port, and I ran a commercial fishing boat out onto Lake Michigan a few times a week when the mood struck me. But mostly we relaxed, getting to know our new community, enjoying our retirement, and watching Charlie's career with pride.

Then one summer evening, I came home from a good day's fishing to find my wife waiting for me on the dock. Her body was tense with emotion and her eyes far away. Something in her attitude triggered a long-buried memory. Before my mind's eye flashed a vision: little towheaded Charlie, age three, slipping on the deck of our sailboat and plunging over the side. I heard again his terrified cries as he flailed in the deep water and felt the chill of the cold water as I dove in beside him and pulled him to safety. The look on my wife's face that day, when she saw little Charlie plunge over the side of our boat, was the same look she had on her face now, and I knew before I reached her that Charlie was dead. He'd been swept overboard in a storm and drowned.

I'm not too sure how we got by in the days that followed. Charlie was our only child, and my wife and I were devastated by his loss. About two weeks after the funeral, I came home from fishing to find my wife standing out on the back deck, her eyes fixed on something in the backyard. She didn't even glance at me as I joined her at the rail; she just pointed toward the water. I followed her gesture and saw a ring-billed seagull standing on the huge, rusted ship's anchor that stood beside the little dock where we kept my wife's sailboat. It had been a gift to us from Charlie, who'd retrieved it from a shipwreck during one of his diving vacations.

There was nothing remarkable about the bird, save for a funny dark-gray patch on one of its light-gray wings. But it stood unnaturally still, and its bright eyes were fixed on us as if it wanted to speak. Like all sailors, I was fond of seagulls. Their bodies are said to contain the souls of drowned sailors who come back to help the living. Whenever a seagull landed on my fishing boat, I took it as a good omen. I'd brought home many a fine catch and sailed safely through many a rough sea accompanied by a seagull companion.

This bird seemed different from the other gulls I'd seen all my life. It was more intense somehow, as if it truly contained a living soul. After considering me for a moment, the seagull opened its beak and cried out plaintively. My heart began beating faster. The seagull's voice sounded just like the voice of my son Charlie.

"It flew right into the house through the front window," my wife said, her voice breaking. "It perched on the back of Charlie's favorite chair and called out to me in Charlie's voice. Then it sailed out the back door and it's been sitting on Charlie's anchor ever since. I think it's been waiting for you to come home."

Hearing her voice, the seagull called again and then flew toward us, settling on the railing. My wife began to tremble. "Charlie?" she whispered. The seagull blinked its eyes at her, bobbed its head once, and then flew in a circle around us before heading out over the lake. It disappeared into the sunset, and my wife sighed softly, as if a weight had lifted from her shoulders.

THE SEAGULL

From that moment, my wife's spirits began to pick up, and a little of the shadow passed from her face.

The seagull with the funny gray patch took up residence on our anchor after that, and my wife took comfort in its presence, often bringing out slices of her homemade bread to feed it after our evening meal. The seagull would accompany her out on the sailboat, and she spoke to it as if it were the spirit of our son Charlie returned to comfort her.

About two months after Charlie's death, I was out fishing by myself a couple of miles offshore when I heard a familiar cry. Looking up, I saw my wife's seagull flying quickly toward me over the choppy waves. It perched on the bow and called out "Ma, Ma," in Charlie's voice. I was alarmed and turned the boat at once, sure that something had happened to my wife. "I'm coming, Charlie," I said to the bird. The seagull bobbed its head and flew back toward shore. I gunned the motor and followed it.

I made it back to the harbor in record time and broke all the speeding laws driving back to the house. I shouted for my wife as I crashed through the front door, but there was no answer. I searched the downstairs for her and then heard the seagull's voice from the backyard: "Ma, Ma!"

I ran out the back door and found my wife unconscious on the ground beneath our deck with the seagull huddled next to her broken right arm. A shattered flowerpot beside her and the broken deck railing above revealed what had happened. I was afraid to move her, so I commanded the seagull to stay with her and ran to telephone for an ambulance. Then the bird and I crouched beside my wife, one on either side of her, until the wail of a siren indicated that help had arrived.

At the hospital, it was found that my wife had sustained severe internal damage from the fall, and she was rushed into surgery. It was a close thing. The doctor told me in the recovery ward that I'd arrived just in time. In another half hour, she would have been too far gone for him to save her.

I didn't get home to my empty house until midnight. Before going to bed, I hurried to Charlie's anchor out back. The seagull was perched there with its head under its wing. It looked up as I approached and called out: "Ma, Ma?"

"Ma's going to be all right," I told it. "Thank you, Charlie."

The bird fluffed its feathers in delight and blinked its eyes several times.

Then it opened its beak and called again. I know it sounds crazy, but I swear there were words in its cry. It sounded like the bird said "Love you. Love you."

Tears sprang to my eyes. "We love you too," I said as the seagull sprang from its perch on the anchor and flew out over the darkened waters of Lake Michigan.

We never saw the seagull again.

My wife recovered fully and came home a month later. To this day, we both believe that Charlie's spirit came back to us for a few weeks to comfort and protect his mother and went away again after he knew she was safe.

8

The Phantom Trespasser

SAGINAW, MICHIGAN

Father was not a man to be trifled with, as we children knew all too well. He was a big rawboned man, with a grizzled head of curly hair and a hearty laugh that could shake the rafters. But he was also a stern disciplinarian, and we learned early on not to cross him. So, when a trespasser started roaming 'round our new house and yard, we knew it would not be long before Father decided to do something.

My brothers had seen the dark-haired, wrinkled old man from time to time, wandering near the house. He wore a Great Lakes captain's uniform, which gave him a rather nautical air. Once I saw him in the kitchen, disappearing through the back door—literally *through* the door, for it was closed at the time. I decided not to mention that incident to Father. He already thought I was a silly girl with a head full of boys and other nonsense. If I told him our trespasser was a lake captain from the Other Realm, he would probably send me away to a convent until I was 40!

Aside from the trespasser, our rambling house was pretty normal, with almost enough bedrooms, a cozy kitchen, and a formal parlor downstairs. We even had a library full of books.

The library was my favorite room. In spite of what Father said, I was far from an "empty-headed" girl. I was a woman with ambitions, and I planned to attend university, even though that was "not done" by the girls in our social circle. I was in my last year of high school, and I studied nearly as often as I checked my hair in the mirror or daydreamed about Harry, the boy who lived across the street.

I'd met Harry on the day we moved to Saginaw. He was studying to be a doctor, and he was almost my beau. That was another thing I didn't mention to Father, for fear he would shoot right through the roof.

Harry was intrigued when I told him about our phantom. Together, we started asking around our neighborhood to see if there had been any unexpected deaths or tragic happenings connected to our house that might explain the ghost. We struck gold when we went to interview the old woman who lived in the house right behind ours. According to Mrs. Smith, a previous owner of the house was a retired Great Lakes ship captain who had died of heart failure in the front parlor. His name was Captain Taylor, and he had been obsessed with his house and its grounds.

"Captain Taylor's spirit comes back to check up on the house every now and again," old Mrs. Smith told me and Harry. "Perhaps you've seen him?" She gave us a knowing smile.

We both nodded eagerly.

"Well, best to leave his ghost alone," Mrs. Smith advised us. "Captain Taylor had a bad temper, and the neighborhood children took care never to vex him. Once he caught a little fellow picking flowers in his front garden and chased the boy all the way down the block. After that, Captain Taylor shouted curses at the little boy every time he passed by until the poor little lad was too scared to walk down the block."

"How terrible," I exclaimed, sitting up indignantly. "What happened next?"

"Well," said Mrs. Smith, "the boy worked up his courage and went to the house to apologize to Captain Taylor for taking his flowers. After that, everything was as right as rain. Captain Taylor never was one to hold a grudge, I'll give him credit for that."

I settled back in my chair and finished eating the cookies Mrs. Smith had given me and Harry. Captain Taylor sounded like a tough old man to me, but no more so than my own father. In fact, I suspected I might have liked him, as long as I was careful to stay on his good side. When we were done eating the cookies, Harry and I thanked Mrs. Smith and went home.

That very same day, Father announced at supper that he'd had enough of our trespasser. He loaded up his rifle around 9:00 p.m. and stalked outside into the growing darkness. I watched through the window as he stumbled and cursed his way into the shrubbery to lay in wait for the prowler. I wondered what he would make of the ghostly sailor, and what Captain Taylor would make of him.

I spent the evening peering out of my upper-story window to see how Father was doing (and to watch the light burning in Harry's bedroom window), so I was the first to see the phantom trespasser when he appeared in the garden. Captain Taylor materialized next to the gate, looking toward the house. As he strolled casually forward, inspecting the well-manicured lawn, Father erupted from the shrubbery with a yell that could have woken the dead. Taking aim with his rifle, Father fired a shot at the phantom. The bullet went right through its translucent body and lodged in a nearby tree. To my surprise, the ghostly Captain Taylor stumbled a bit and clutched at his arm, as if the bullet had stung him. He gave Father an angry glare, then he vanished into thin air with a small popping noise like the sound of a cork coming out of a wine bottle.

Inside the house, my mother was exclaiming in fright over the gunshot, and my brothers were cheering and running down the staircase to the front hall. The boys wholeheartedly supported Father's method of dealing with trespassers, and they were at an age that anything having to do with blood and gore appealed to them mightily. I followed my family out onto the porch. To my surprise, I found Harry there, beating the bushes with Father. Harry had come running when he heard the rifle shot, and Father had dragooned him into searching for the man that he'd "winged" with his rifle. Father searched the grounds for nearly an hour but found no sign of Captain Taylor. I took Harry aside privately and showed him the tree in which Father's bullet had lodged. We decided not to tell Father that he'd shot a ghost.

The next evening, the phantom trespasser returned with a vengeance. The whole household was awakened from sleep by a thunderous banging on the walls, which moved from one room to the next, upstairs and down, all night long. Father chased the sound around and around, looking rather ludicrous in his long gray nightshirt and cap, a glowing lantern clutched in one hand. Sometimes he rapped the wall right where the spirit was knocking and ordered it to come out and "fight like a man." Between the ghost's antics and Father's shouting, we didn't get much sleep that night.

THE PHANTOM TRESPASSER

In the days that followed, the ghostly Captain Taylor appeared to escort us out of the yard every time any one of us left the house. I didn't mind a bit since the fellow doffed his hat to me and behaved in a very gentlemanlike fashion. He was courteous to Mother too, and he shadowboxed with my two young brothers, much to their delight. He seemed altogether solid when he was in the shade. It was only when he stepped into bright sunlight that we could see through him. He even bowed to Harry when my beau came home from his summer job. Harry was taken aback at the sight of the phantom, whom he had heard about but never before seen. But he recovered quickly and bowed back politely, remembering what Mrs. Smith had told us about the ghost's fiery temper.

It was a completely different story with Father. As soon as he stepped from the porch, the phantom would appear with a martial light in his eye. He would silently rant at Father and dog his steps out into the street. Father took to peering anxiously through a window before he left the house, and then he'd make for the road at a dead run. His strategy never varied, and it never worked. My brothers and I found the whole situation hilarious, though we smothered our giggles with our hands lest Father hear us and tan our hides for the crime of disrespect. Even Mother's lips twitched when Father began his ritual for leaving the house.

In the hours after supper, we'd gather in the parlor to relax and read. Sometimes the phantom trespasser would join us, though he remained mostly invisible. I could see his hands, which he would teasingly pass between my eyes and book as he passed by my chair with a soft puff of chilly wind. My brothers would exclaim and giggle when he did the same to them, and

Father would glare at them for disturbing his reading. A few moments later, Father would shout aloud with annoyance when the ghostly Captain Taylor played the same joke on him, and Mother would tell him to hush and sit down before he disturbed the neighbors. Though her voice was stern, her eyes twinkled merrily at me once Father returned to reading.

When Father was alone in the parlor, the tricks played by the phantom trespasser accelerated. Newspapers were tweaked out of his hand, the fire in the stove would go out abruptly, or the lights would wink off and on. Father stopped using the parlor altogether unless another family member was with him. And woe betide us if we left the room long enough for the phantom trespasser to pull any tricks.

Nights were particularly trying because we never knew if we were going to get any sleep. Some nights were peaceful, but others were full of rapping and rumbling and an occasional bang that interrupted our slumber and made Father run around and around in bare feet with his nightcap askew.

News of our ghost had spread through the neighborhood, though it was rare that anyone outside the family could see him, even when he stood directly in front of their noses. Harry could see him, but I believe this was because the phantom knew Harry was my beau and considered him one of the family.

One evening, Father invited a number of his skeptical friends to spend the night in our guest room to experience our ghost firsthand. The phantom trespasser was very obliging that night, whipping newspapers from shaking hands, banging on the walls, and sending the skeptics running for their lives.

The phantom may have enjoyed himself hugely that evening, but Mother had had enough. She confronted Father in the kitchen the next morning right after breakfast. Though my brothers and I listened at the door, we could not make out exactly what she said to him in her low, furious voice. Whatever it was, it had an instant effect.

Scowling fiercely, Father marched out the front door, down into the yard, and apologized to the ghost of Captain Taylor, who had appeared as usual the moment Father's foot touched the front porch. It was a fulsome apology indeed, starting with his inexcusably rude behavior in shooting Captain Taylor and ending with his subsequent inhospitable and offensive manner. The tone and the words sounded more like those used by Mother, but Father's contrition was sincere, and the phantom trespasser seemed to know it. When Father finished speaking, the ghostly Captain Taylor grasped his hand and shook it enthusiastically. Then he waved to my brothers and me, who were watching from the porch, and marched down the front walk, vanishing when he reached the road.

I told Harry the whole story when he came over after work. "I'm afraid that's the last we'll see of the phantom trespasser," I said with a sigh. I'd grown fond of our ghost, despite his antics.

"Not necessarily," Harry predicted with a smile.

And he was right. The nocturnal noises and the parlor tricks ceased after Father apologized to Captain Taylor's ghost. But the phantom trespasser would still occasionally appear in the yard near our house, bowing to Mother and me, shadowboxing with the boys, and nodding politely to Father, which made me glad.

9

A Father's Revenge

DETROIT, MICHIGAN

He watched uneasily as his only child—a fair daughter—laughed as she traded goods with the handsome white trapper who came to their village each week with his skins. His girl-child was very shy and spoke little even to the people she had known all her life. But now she was glowing as she exchanged soft words with the white man with fair hair and sky-blue eyes. The father did not like what he saw, but what could he say? His daughter did nothing wrong, said nothing unseemly. She just smiled a little too brightly at the trapper's wit and charm as they traded goods.

When the young man was gone, he asked his daughter about her conversation with the white man. What topic fascinated her so? She turned her bright eyes to her old father, who was chief of his village and whom she loved with her whole heart. "We spoke about life," she said, "about the sun and the stars and the many beautiful things that surround us."

The old chief knew in that moment that his only child was in love with the white man. He knew there was nothing he could say that would change the desire in her heart, so he just touched her cheek gently and walked away. But he did not hold himself as proudly as before, and his sloping shoulders revealed his worry to those who knew him well. His daughter might once have noticed such a change, but now there were stars in her eyes, and she saw nothing but a vision of the handsome face and supple form of the young trapper.

The old chief knew that the young couple was meeting in the meadow outside the village, spending many days walking in the woods and talking. His daughter did not neglect her duties to her father during this time. His meals were served on time, and his clothing was kept clean. But the girl went about her daily tasks with a distracted air, and the old chief knew she was eager to finish her work so she could go to the meadow and see her love.

One day he said to his only daughter, "My child, I will lose you soon, I think."

His daughter blushed happily and nodded. "Yes, Father. We were going to ask you for permission to marry as soon as possible. Thomas wants both you and the priest to marry us, so we are bound both by our laws and his."

The old chief nodded, pleased by this news. So, the young trapper was serious. Thomas would not take his only daughter as a plaything but would give her the rank and status she deserved.

"You see," his daughter said playfully. "You should not have worried."

The chief smiled and told his daughter to bring her young man to meet with him the next time Thomas came to the village. She promised this gladly and hummed as she cleared away his meal.

The next morning, the old chief was passing through the wood beside the meadow when he heard his daughter's voice raised in protest. He picked up his pace in alarm, and then stopped when he heard the young trapper's voice.

"Father Constantine said it would be a sin for us to marry," Thomas repeated. "I told him that you would join the church, but he said it did not matter. He said no one will accept us or our children because I am white, and you are not."

"You told me that your God was not a white man," the girl replied. "That the one you worship lived and died in a land far across the sea, where men's skins are as dark as mine. If this is so, how can your God look down upon one such as I?"

The trapper would not listen. He repeated Father Constantine's words until the girl was silenced. The old chief trembled with rage, his anger directed more at the friar who had counseled the troubled boy than against the boy himself. He wanted to shake the lad, to tell Thomas to follow his heart and not the words of the priest, but the old chief knew that it was not his place. He had not interfered with the beginning of his daughter's romance, and he would not interfere with its end.

"I am sorry," he heard Thomas saying over and over, as his daughter began to weep. "I am sorry."

The old chief could not bear to hear his daughter crying, and so he moved silently away, returning to his home by another route so his daughter would not see him.

Later, his daughter came into their home silently. Her head averted, she made his meal without once looking at him. His heart was wrung with pain at the sight of her grief, and finally he spoke. "Speak to me, daughter," he said. "Tell me what troubles you."

"Thomas is going away," she said, addressing her words to the fire. "We will not be married after all."

"My poor child," the old chief said quietly, his voice choking on the words.

His daughter nodded in acknowledgment, but she did not speak again.

When the old chief woke the next morning, the fire had gone out and there was no sign of his daughter. He sat up abruptly, his heart pounding in fear, and then ran out into the village, clothing askew and hair awry, to search for her. He turned his feet at last toward the river, and then stopped when he saw a huddle of people at the top of the incline, looking down into the pool below. They glanced up when they heard his running feet and then turned away, unable to meet his eyes. He went to the top of the slope and looked down at the slight figure floating face down in the water, her long, dark hair swirling softly around her drowned form.

The old chief did not feel himself fall to his knees, nor was he aware of screaming his daughter's name over and over in agony. He saw nothing save the vision of his child's body drifting there in the water. It was his oldest friend who finally pulled him to his feet and helped him back to his home.

From that moment forward, the only thought in the old chief's mind was that of revenge. He wanted to kill the young trapper who had driven his child to her death, but Thomas had already set out for the East, never to return. So, the old chief's hatred turned instead to Father Constantine.

The old chief wasted no time. That night he crept into the friar's room and silently slid a knife into the man's heart. His presence at the fort passed unnoticed, and Father Constantine's body was not discovered until noon of the following day. The

A FATHER'S REVENGE

whole fort was shocked. The guards were doubled and trebled, but no one knew who killed the good Father, or why.

For a few days, the old chief was at peace. Although he mourned his daughter and turned his duties over to a young cousin who would one day soon be chief, he relished the thought that he had avenged his daughter's death. But gradually, the old chief became aware of a voice calling to him in the wind. Over and over, it spoke his name reproachfully. Finally, the chief recognized the voice of Father Constantine.

"Why did you kill me?" the voice whispered through the treetops during the early evening hours. "Murderer!" it shrieked at the height of a windstorm. The old chief did his best to ignore the voice, chanting prayers and meditating, but the voice only grew louder and more persistent.

"Why did you kill me?" the wind whistled under his blanket at night. "Murderer!" it shouted through the meadow grasses at noon.

Then the tolling of the bells began. *Bong. Bong. Bong.* These were the great bells of the fort, which called the white men to Mass each week. *Bong. Bong. Bong.* But it was the wrong day and the wrong time for Mass. The old chief was confused, and he asked his young cousin why the bells were ringing. His cousin looked at him strangely and very gently told the old chief that no bells had sounded that day.

Still, the old chief heard them ringing, hour after hour, ringing in counterpoint to the voice in the wind shrieking, "Murderer! Murderer!"

Unable to eat, unable to sleep, the old chief sat beside a blackened fire, wrapped in a dirty blanket, shaking and rocking and humming to himself to drown out the voices and the tolling of the bells. Hour after hour his people tried to speak to him, to comfort him, but he was beyond their reach. Still, they loved their old chief, and so all the women and many of the men in the tribe took turns sitting with him, trying to tempt him back to life with delicious food and soft conversation.

The chief sat in silent agony for a week. Then on Sunday morning, the real bells of Mass began to toll. At the sound, the old chief abruptly stopped rocking. He sat up straight and stared into the face of his cousin's wife, whose countenance he saw clearly for the first time in days.

"Tell my cousin to be a good chief," he said to the woman. Then he rose, threw off his blanket, and started running toward the fort. His people called out in amazement and followed him, but he ran with supernatural speed and quickly outdistanced them.

As the last toll of the final bell faded into silence, the old chief burst through the doors of the church and ran straight up to the altar. Tall and proud and angry, he turned to face the congregation. "It was I who killed Father Constantine," he said. "I stole into your fort in the night and took his life because he stole the life of my child, my only daughter! It was he who sent her lover away because her skin was not white, and she took her own life because of the friar's false counsel. Father Constantine was no better than a murderer, and so I punished him for his crime!"

The old chief stopped abruptly, overcome suddenly with weakness and a terrible pain in his left arm. He stood swaying in agony as the congregation exclaimed in horror. Several soldiers who were attending the early Mass leapt to their feet and approached him cautiously.

Ignoring them, the old chief turned to look at the priest who had come to replace Father Constantine. "I, too, am a murderer," the old chief said, "and I deserve to die because I took the life of a holy man. I realize this now."

The priest stared down at him, shock and pity on his gentle, intelligent face.

"Pray for me," the old chief whispered to the priest as he fell slowly to the floor of the church. By the time the soldiers reached him, he was dead.

10

Red Rover

TOLEDO, OHIO

I took command of the *Red Rover* shortly after Captain Shaughnessy was killed on Ten Mile Creek just below Toledo. The *Rover* was a good ship, very sturdy, and we ran cargo all over Lake Erie. We made a good profit, and I was pleased with my new command.

But as the months went by, I became convinced that my crew and I were not the only ones aboard the ship. It usually happened at dusk, when I stood on deck watching the stars slowly fill the night sky. I'd feel a presence standing beside me, watching night fall over the massive lake. As the gulls settled on the water and the shoreline disappeared in the darkness, I sometimes saw a shadow that was darker than the air around it. It was the outline of a man in a captain's uniform and hat.

"Shaughnessy, is that you?" I whispered one evening to the shadow figure beside the mast. A small breeze whipped around me, almost blowing off my hat. I clapped a hand to save it and glared at the shadow by the mast. It vanished. I marched away a bit too briskly, heart pounding with supernatural dread.

After a calming drink in my cabin, I decided there was nothing harmful about the shadow figure. Shaughnessy was just watching over the *Red Rover*, same as he'd done in life. But I decided not to mention it to the mate or any of the crew. Sailors were a superstitious lot.

We were on a cargo run to the north of the lake, sailing against a mighty headwind, when the mate sang out, "Captain, we've sprung a leak!" It was a serious one. More than a foot of water was already inside the hold, and it was rising too fast for my liking. If this kept up, we'd be on the bottom in no time, and most of the crew couldn't swim.

"Man the pumps," I said briskly, and the crew set to.

With everyone working flat out, we were able to make headway against the rising water level, but we couldn't stop the leak. I thought we could save the *Rover* (and ourselves), but we'd have to keep the leak under control and limp her to port as fast as we could safely go. When the water was down far enough, I ordered a break. The men flopped to the floor, gasping for breath. We watched tensely as the water crept back up. I'd kept my eye on a knot in the wood, reckoning we could wait until the water reached it before pumping again. At nine minutes, water was lapping at the knot. I ordered everyone back on the pumps.

We alternated pumping with 10-minute breaks for many hours, while the mate and a skeleton crew kept us sailing toward harbor. At first, I tried putting the men into shifts to give them more time to rest, but the water rose too fast. We had to pump with all available hands, making do as best we could with 10-minute breaks.

Hours later, with the *Red Rover* still fighting its way through the stubborn wind and large waves, I called a short halt and sent the men to lie down in their bunks. I would let them rest for 20 minutes this time. It would put us behind, but the men would collapse if they continued at this pace.

I sat on the edge of my bunk with my timepiece, glad to rest for a moment. I stared blearily at the face of my pocket watch. Twenty minutes. No more. Just 20 minutes . . .

Someone grabbed me painfully by the hair, jerking me awake. I was dragged out of bed and thrown to the floor. My scalp burned with pain. I reached up and felt a bald patch where the hair had been completely torn out. What in the name of . . . ?

I scrambled to my feet, roaring with anger. There was no one in my cabin and no running footsteps from a fleeing intruder. I heard nothing except wind and waves and snoring from the crew's quarters. Wait, that wasn't right. The leak! The pumps!

I panicked, reaching for my pocket watch. I'd been so exhausted, I'd fallen asleep. For how long? Were we swamped? Was the ship going down?

I found the watch in the bedclothes and opened it with trembling fingers. Dear Lord. We'd been asleep for nearly three hours. We were doomed! I couldn't believe we weren't already at the bottom of the lake.

I bellowed for the crew and heard them falling out of the bunks, swearing as they realized we'd overslept. Everyone raced for the hold, expecting every second to find ourselves wading waist deep in water. The hold was empty of water. We skidded to a halt, staring in amazement. How could this be? The skeleton crew had no time to come down and pump, even if they'd known about the extended break. Had the leak sealed itself? That was impossible.

At that moment, a translucent figure appeared directly behind the closest pump and gestured sternly at me, indicating

RED ROVER

that the sailors should work the pumps. The message was clear: I've done enough. It's your turn.

I realized it was the ghost of Captain Shaughnessy who pulled me from my bunk just now. He had saved our lives by manning the pumps for three hours while we slept. The phantom bowed slightly to me and vanished.

"Holy Mary, Mother of God," breathed a sailor, grabbing for his rosary. Apparently, I wasn't the only one who could see the captain's ghost.

Glancing toward the corner with the leak, I saw that a pool of water was forming. It was not pouring in like before, but we would still need to keep sailors on the pumps until we reached port.

"What are you waiting for?" I said briskly, gesturing at the incoming water. "Someone take care of that."

"Aye, aye," gasped a sailor. His words broke the spell. They leapt into action, some to man the pumps and some to relieve the busy skeleton crew.

I found the first mate at the helm. He had kept us on course this whole while, not knowing that the rest of the crew had overslept while a ghost manned the pumps. I sent the mate to rest and took over the helm, while the rested sailors relieved their comrades. I could hear the men whispering all around me and knew the ghost story was making the rounds of the ship.

When we reached harbor, the crew unloaded the cargo as fast as humanly possible. Then, to a man, they abandoned ship. No one wanted to work aboard a haunted vessel. I didn't blame them. I grabbed my own belongings and walked off the *Red Rover* at their heels. After reporting the leak—and the ghost—to the proper authorities, I resigned my commission and got out of town. I was grateful to the former Captain Shaughnessy for saving our lives, but I wasn't willing to share my command with anyone, dead or alive. I'd head over to Buffalo and find me a brand-new ship to captain. One without a ghost.

Memorial

PUT-IN-BAY, OHIO

I was in the mood for a spooky adventure, so I took the ferry over to Put-in-Bay to pay a visit to the supposedly haunted Perry Memorial. A strong wind out of Canada was blowing across the lake, so I ducked into the sheltered passenger room to get out of the cold breeze. Beneath me, the big car ferry tossed almost alarmingly from side to side as it crossed to South Bass Island under a lowering sky. I found it exhilarating, but much colder than the weather had forecasted. I was in short sleeves without a coat. I would need to buy a souvenir sweatshirt at Put-in-Bay.

I walked off the ferry and found my way to the local "taxi." For three dollars plus tip, I was driven to the center of town by a nice local woman who told me a little bit about the island. From the drop-off point, I made my way to the Perry's Victory and International Peace Memorial and watched a 15-minute video about Commodore Oliver Hazard Perry and his role in the War of 1812. Fought on September 10, 1813, the Battle of Lake Erie took place off the coast of Ohio not far from Put-in-Bay. Nine vessels of the United States Navy under the command of Commodore Perry defeated and captured six vessels of the British Royal Navy. It was a terrible fight with many casualties on both sides. But in the end, Perry's naval victory ensured American control of the lake for the rest of the war, which allowed the Americans to recover Detroit and win the Battle of the Thames. It was one of the biggest naval battles of the War of 1812 and a decisive victory that eventually led to a lasting peace between the United States, Canada, and Great Britain.

After the film, I walked across lush green grass toward the 352-foot-tall column. Despite the dark clouds massing overhead, the memorial didn't look haunted. The wind howled across the lawn, bending the tops of the trees and seriously interfering with the flight path of some swooping swallows. I grew colder by the minute, but had thriftily resisted buying an expensive sweatshirt in the gift shop. Instead, I hurried up the steps and into the relatively sheltered bottom floor of the memorial column, where the bodies of the British and American command staff were buried. I took a few pictures on my cell phone and huddled for a moment next to a vent giving off puffs of warm air. Then the wind found its way through one of the open doors, urging me up the stairs to the supposedly haunted (but hopefully warmer) second floor. The rounded room on the second floor had a big central elevator to take tourists to the top. It was rumored that dark figures haunted the staircase to the locked floor above my head. And a ghost supposedly played tricks with the velvet ropes near the elevator. I saw the ropes, but no ghosts were visible—at least to my eyes—as I waited in line for the elevator.

Two friendly park employees examined my national parks pass and then gave me leave to store my backpack with them while I explored the observation deck. I went up the old-fashioned elevator with a family from San Antonio, Texas.

The mother commented on my short sleeves and commiserated with me about the cold weather. Still, we soldiered on, heading through the door at the top and straight into a heavy wind.

The observation deck had amazing vistas of the islands, but between the cold and wind I couldn't be up here very long. I zoomed around the tower, taking random scenic photos before pausing to ask the employee stationed on the deck to show me where the naval battle took place in the waterscape below. He kindly filled me in on the details, and I fixed the sight in my mind before hurrying into the sheltered room to line up for the next elevator. If there were any ghostly murmurings on the observation deck, the wind had completely obliviated them.

Back on the haunted floor, I thanked the staff, grabbed my bag, and headed downstairs. All spooky thoughts were obliterated by my shivers. I didn't care how much it cost, I was buying a sweatshirt in the gift shop at the visitor center before I froze to death in this howling wind. But when I stepped inside, I found the building invaded by a class from a local school. There was no pushing my way through the crowd, so I retreated back the way I came. I'd have to purchase a sweatshirt from a gift shop in town.

I barely glanced at the memorial as I speed-walked past the velvety tulips nodding in the brisk breeze. As I turned toward the parking lot, I heard a voice calling: "Excuse me, miss."

I turned in surprise just as I was hailed a second time by a man wearing a War of 1812 naval officer's uniform, typical of the ones I'd seen earlier in the film. He stood near one of the young trees flanking the parking lot. My eyes widened. He looked like a historical reenactor, come to deliver a speech to the young scholars inside the building. Except that he wasn't

MEMORIAL

solid! If you looked carefully, you could see the grass and the bark of the tree through his uniform.

I was already chilled to the bone in the breeze off the lake, so I couldn't tell if the gooseflesh on my body was from the phantom officer or from the wind. It didn't matter. His face was kind, and he was speaking politely to me. So I greeted him and asked what he wanted.

"Do you have any questions about the battle?" he asked me. Before I could answer, he continued, "It was hellish. Much worse than any film could possibly describe." So he told me about it in his own words.

"We cheered, you know, when Perry raised his secret flag," he began. "It said: 'Don't Give Up The Ship,' and we were determined to honor that sentiment. But we were scared. Dear God, I was shaking in my boots. There's nowhere to run, you know, in a naval battle. Except for the water, and like most sailors, I cannot swim."

He shook his head and rubbed his face with his hand. He continued, "You wait and wait for the battle to start, and that's almost the worst bit. Then the first cannon shot is fired, and you are filled with the terrible energy of war, running to and fro on a deck that seemed large until the battle began. Now it feels too small, and there's smoke everywhere, and the acrid stench gags you. You dodge debris and steady the cannon and give orders and watch your men die, one after another, right in front of you."

As the officer spoke, I pictured the flashes as the cannon fired, smelled the acrid smoke, heard the sharp cries of the injured and dying. My heartbeat accelerated as he continued.

"The noise is deafening as the cannons fire over and over. You are struck by flying debris, and wood splinters come at you like spears whenever a cannonball bursts through the side of the ship or hits the wood of the deck. One of my men was killed by a huge splinter that drilled into his skull after a cannonball hit the side of the ship."

The officer told me there was blood everywhere. It covered the deck of the ship and his clothes and hands. One side of his body was burning hot from the heat of the firing cannon, and the other freezing cold from the wind chilling the sweat on his straining body. His coat was in tatters from the splinters and shrapnel flying everywhere. He saw a marine private's legs blown off by a cannon blast. He was slipping and sliding toward the injured man on a deck slick with blood when he felt a sudden searing pain, followed by blackness.

"The pain stopped as abruptly as it came," he continued. "I felt peace and heard an indescribably lovely voice calling my name. I opened my eyes and saw a glowing figure holding out its hand toward me, telling me to come away." The officer bowed his head for a moment, and I stood fighting tears as he described his own death.

The officer looked up and saw my tears. "Don't cry," he said. "It was a terrible battle, but we won. Perry had four of our men row him to the *Niagara* after the *Lawrence* was incapacitated. He sailed the *Niagara* right into the middle of the British fleet, which was in disarray after the loss of key officers. We fought them to a standstill. It was a great victory. And the peace that came afterward made it worth the sacrifice." He gestured toward the peace memorial and smiled.

"Thank you for telling me about the battle," I said, wiping my eyes. "I'm sorry that you . . . died."

"But not in vain," he said. "Not in vain."

He bowed abruptly and vanished, just as the doors to the visitor center swung open and a bevy of schoolchildren entered the grounds. It was disconcerting. I'd been transported to September 1813 as the officer spoke, and now I was back in the twenty-first century, not sure if my shivers were from my ghostly encounter or from the cold breeze. As the schoolchildren headed toward the memorial, I gazed across the lake in the direction of the battle. For a moment, I could picture the navy ships firing upon one another, feel the boom of cannon, smell the acrid smoke, hear the cries of the dying. Then an emphatic breeze swirled about me, bringing me back to the present. I shivered, rubbing my chilled skin. I'd wanted a spooky experience and, boy, had I gotten one. Now I needed a dose of normal. And a sweatshirt. One of those would be easy to find.

Back in the empty visitor center, I swiftly found what I was looking for in the gift shop. A navy-blue long-sleeved shirt with the phrase "Don't Give Up The Ship" printed on the front was just my size. My skin prickled, remembering the words of the phantom soldier. "We cheered when Perry raised the flag." I purchased the shirt and slipped into the bathroom to put it on. Satisfied by this nod to the past, I walked through the town square, had a salad for lunch, and took the bus back to the ferry and my hotel, done with spooky adventures, at least for today.

12

Sudden Snow

CLEVELAND, OHIO

Most of the town turned out to help a neighbor clear part of the forest so he could build a cabin for his son and the girl he would take as his new bride. It was a happy but exhausting day, cutting down huge trees, sawing them into useable segments, and using teams of horses to drag them out of the clearing. Some would be used in the construction of the cabin. Some would go to the sawmill to be sold, and the money would help the young couple set up housekeeping. More than one of us had worked in a logging camp, so we were old hands at clearing a strip.

At midday, the ladies set out an amazing spread and we feasted until I wasn't sure we'd have energy to keep working. The soon-to-be-bride fried some apple tarts that were even better than the ones my mama used to make. We spent the afternoon teasing the young man about his talented bride-to-be 'til he blushed happily and told us to hush up.

Several neighbors offered me a ride home, but I refused. I loved walking the autumn woods at night, listening to the owls hooting and watching the moon rise among the endless sweep of stars overhead. I sighed happily, for I had a fry pie in each pocket, set aside for me by the bride-to-be when she saw how much I loved them. As I munched on pies, I designed a special pair of rocking chairs I'd make the couple as a wedding gift.

It was 9 p.m. and I was nearly home when a man suddenly appeared in the middle of the moonlit road about a dozen yards in front of me. The man was surrounded by heavily falling snow. Wind gusted the snow every which way so the man couldn't see, and he struggled through knee-deep drifts with shoulders hunched and head down. I'd never seen such a massive squall, even working the lumber camps in northern Canada.

I stopped in my tracks, staring in amazement at the scene before me. I stood in bright, leaf-spangled moonlight, the air around me crisp but not cold. Yet right in front of me, a man was caught in the worst snowstorm I'd ever seen. I rubbed my eyes and blinked. When I looked again, the man was still there, still struggling to find his way through the snowstorm. I shivered, disconcerted by the strangeness of this situation. Then a thought struck me. Maybe I was supposed to help him. I gave a holler, but the man didn't answer me. I saw him fall to the ground in exhaustion, snow pummeling his still form where it lay. Forget the strange circumstances. That man needed help! I ran to save him.

As I drew level with the swirling snowstorm, I saw the man give two or three desperate gasps and then lie still. I thrust my way into the phantom storm. It was icy cold. Ghostly snow swirled all around me but I felt neither gusting wind nor snowy wetness. The air was heavy, and it resisted me. I felt as if I were truly fighting my way through deep snowdrifts as I struggled to reach the dying man. I dropped to my knees beside him and gasped in shocked recognition. The white face belonged to my

SUDDEN SNOW

mother's brother, who lived in Dakota Territory, about two thousand miles from our home on Lake Erie.

"Uncle John," I cried, "please wake up! We need to get you out of this storm." I reached for him, ready to lift him onto my shoulder and carry him home. But Uncle John vanished, storm and all. I was left kneeling in the moonlight on an empty stretch of road less than a mile from my home.

I pulled myself up and wobbled homeward on legs that would hardly carry me. What had I just seen? What did it mean? My wife took one look at my face and dosed me good with some patent medicine she got from a bottle she bought when the traveling grocery man came through town last week. She was almost as shaken up as I was when she heard my story. We were sure that something terrible had happened, but there wasn't anything we could do about it.

The vision I'd seen gave both of us a bad feeling for days afterward. Even the arrival of a thank-you basket filled with fresh-baked apple-fry pies (complete with attached recipe) from the bride-to-be and her groom couldn't erase the memory.

Three weeks after the logging bee, my wife met me at the door with a strained look on her face and a letter in her hand. "It's from your Aunt Jane," she said. I swallowed and took the envelope from her. We both knew what news it would contain. I sat at the kitchen table and read the short letter aloud.

My dear nephew.

I have sad news. Your Uncle John was walking home from work on the fifth day of this month when he was overtaken by an unexpected autumn blizzard and froze to death in the storm. We had to wait until the ground melted to have the funeral, which took place yesterday at the church in our settlement. The boys and I plan to stay on the ranch for a month or two and see how things go before we make any permanent plans. I will keep you informed of any changes to our situation or address.

Your loving Aunt Jane.

If you calculated the difference in times between Dakota Territory and Cleveland, the date and hour of Uncle John's death exactly matched the date and hour I'd seen his spirit struggling through the phantom snowstorm in the middle of the road.

The White Lady

ROCHESTER, NEW YORK

I must have tried on 10 outfits before I finally decided what I was going to wear on my very first date with Jeff. I had been on the phone all afternoon with one friend after the other, discussing colors, accessories, nail polish, and all the other style essentials that I normally don't think about, since I consider myself an intellectual rather than a fashion plate. But that was before I was asked out by the most popular boy in school.

I went out on the front porch to polish my toenails. I was a third of the way through when a familiar shadow blocked the warm spring sunshine for a moment. I didn't even look up.

"What is it now, Stan?" I asked wearily. My neighbor since birth shuffled his way into the wicker chair next to mine.

"Listen, Jamie, is it true Jeff is taking you on a picnic to Durand-Eastman Park?"

Good grief, I thought. Jeff had just made the final arrangements with me half an hour ago. I had, of course, immediately phoned my best friend, Diane, and told her the news. Assuming it took Diane at least 10 minutes to call all our other friends, and then another 10 minutes for them to call their friends, that would mean that the news must have reached

Stan within 25 minutes after I hung up with Jeff. That had to be some kind of gossiping record, I concluded, looking over at Stan.

Stan looks a bit like a sandy-haired scarecrow. He's 6 feet 2 inches and naturally plays basketball, but outside the court he appears a bit awkward, as if he has two left feet. Stan is also an intellectual, like me. I consider him a good friend, except for his irritating habit of asking me to go out with him at least once a month. I mean, I like Stan, but just as a friend.

"We are going to the park," I answered his question. "Why?"

"I think you should ask Jeff to take you to the movies," said Stan. "The park is a bad idea."

"What do you mean, a bad idea?" I asked suspiciously. Now what was Stan up to? Was he trying to break my date with Jeff?

"Come on, Jamie, even you must have heard about the White Lady," Stan said.

I stared at Stan incredulously for a moment, and then started to laugh. "For a second there, I thought you were serious," I gasped. "The White Lady! For goodness' sake, Stan, no one believes that old story!"

Stan frowned and I stopped laughing. He couldn't be serious! But apparently, he was.

The White Lady was the most famous ghost in the Rochester area. In the early 1800s, the White Lady and her daughter were supposed to have lived on the land where Durand-Eastman Park now stands. Then one day, the daughter disappeared. Convinced that the girl had been harmed and killed by a local farmer, the mother, accompanied by her two German shepherds, searched the marshy lands day after day for her child's body. She never found a trace of her daughter and finally, in her grief, committed suicide. Her faithful dogs pined for their mistress after her death, and soon followed her to the grave. The mother's spirit returned to continue the search for her child. People say that on foggy nights, the White Lady and her dogs rise from Durand Lake. Together, they roam through the park, looking for the missing daughter and seeking vengeance against men. Any man who catches the ghost's eye had best beware, for the White Lady and her dogs are killers. Or at least that's the version of the story I heard at school.

"Come on, Stan. You don't really believe there is a White Lady," I said. "I mean, ghosts? Please!"

"I would still feel much better about the whole thing if you and Jeff went to the movies," Stan said stubbornly.

"I'm touched by your concern," I said sarcastically. "But I am sure we will be just fine. Now, I have to go change. Jeff is picking me up at 6:30."

I left Stan sitting morosely on my porch and went to prepare for my date.

Jeff pulled into my driveway promptly at 6:30 p.m. in his yellow convertible. He was polite and polished with my parents, assuring them he would have me home by curfew, and then he tucked me into the front seat next to him. I could smell fried chicken coming from the picnic basket.

Stan was sitting in a rocker on his porch, watching us as we drove off. Jeff nodded stiffly to him; Stan nodded back.

"I didn't know you lived next door to Stan," Jeff said.

"All my life," I said. Just then my cell phone rang. I answered it, and Stan said, "Tell Jeff that you want to go to the movies."

"Give me a break, Stan," I said, and hung up.

Jeff glanced over at me. "What did Stan want?" he asked.

"Stan thinks we should go to the movies instead of to the park," I explained. "He thinks the White Lady will come and get us if we go there."

Jeff laughed. "I didn't think Stan was so superstitious!" he said. "Or is he jealous?" he asked, glancing at me again.

"I don't know!" I said impishly. "Maybe!"

We laughed and talked all the way to the park. Jeff parked the car in the lot next to Lake Ontario, and we crossed the street to what he called "the White Lady's castle," which overlooks both Lake Ontario and the smaller Lake Durand, a lovely, tree-shrouded lake directly across the street from Lake Ontario. We climbed up the stairs and spread the blanket out on the grassy spot at the top, behind the cobblestone wall. I unpacked the picnic basket, and we sat munching fried chicken and comparing notes about our teachers. Then Jeff started making some sly, rather uncomplimentary remarks about Stan, which I didn't appreciate. I guess he didn't like Stan calling me and telling me not to go to the park. When I didn't respond to his witticism, Jeff changed the subject, embarking upon a monologue of his athletic exploits, which, frankly, bored me to tears. Jeff was really cute, but I prefer my guys to have a bit more modesty than Jeff was currently displaying.

It was dusk when I heard a crashing noise and a familiar muffled cursing coming from the trees behind us. I knew at once that it was Stan. Jeff looked around.

"What was that?" he asked lazily.

"Just some kids fooling around," I said, glaring at Stan, who retreated behind a tree. *Go home*, I mouthed at him and turned to smile at Jeff.

"Fooling around, eh?" Jeff said, giving me a wicked grin. "Sounds like fun!"

Jeff leaned toward me, and I jumped up and walked over to the right side of the wall to look out at Durand Lake. I wasn't going to kiss that vain bore, even to get back at Stan.

To my right, the mist was rising off Durand Lake and the light was growing dim. I could see Stan scrambling down the hill toward the lake as silently as he could. He looked upset, but it served him right for following me on my date. Then I heard a step behind me and Jeff slid his arms around my waist.

"What's the matter, Jamie? Are you playing hard to get?" he asked, nuzzling my neck.

I was watching the mist over the lake, which was swirling strangely. I blinked a few times and suddenly realized that I was seeing a beautiful woman solidifying before my eyes. Two smaller swirls beside her became German shepherds. The White Lady was watching Stan, who had just reached the road at the bottom of the hill. She did not look happy to see him. Stan did not look happy to see her either. For a moment, my neighbor and the ghost stared at one another. The dogs at her side bristled, baring their teeth at him. Then the ghost gestured to the dogs and they ran toward Stan. Stan hightailed it back up the slope as fast as he could go, the ghost dogs snapping at his heels. The White Lady's face transformed from that of a beautiful woman to that of a haggard witch. She started rising up from the surface of the lake, following the crashing sounds Stan was making as he ran up the hill.

"Don't be so shy," Jeff said, nuzzling my hair.

Just then, the White Lady caught a glimpse of me and Jeff cuddled up next to the wall. Stan was forgotten in an instant.

THE WHITE LADY

I stiffened as the ghost, accompanied by her two dogs, started rushing toward us! Feeling me tense, Jeff looked up and saw the White Lady for the first time. He let go of me so fast that I fell against the wall. Jeff didn't even notice. He was too busy stumbling backward, gasping swear words, and falling over the picnic basket. I was frozen to the spot, praying that the stories about the White Lady were true, and that she protected females rather than killing them. The White Lady ignored me completely. I ducked as she sailed right over my head in a rush of freezing cold air. She was aiming for Jeff with a look of murder on her face, and Jeff didn't wait around. He flew around the wall and half-ran, half-stumbled down the stairs, the White Lady on his heels.

I grabbed my cell phone and ran to the top of the steps just as two enormous, semitransparent German shepherds flew across the wall in pursuit of their mistress. I jumped out of their way and watched Jeff running across the road and down the hill toward Lake Ontario, the White Lady and her dogs in hot pursuit. I flipped open my cell phone, started to dial 9-1-1, then paused. The emergency staff would think I was a kook if I reported a malicious ectoplasm chasing my date into the lake. Who *do* you call when a ghost gets out of hand?

Jeff plunged into the lake and submerged. The White Lady floated over the place he disappeared, looking very upset and very determined.

Just then, I heard someone call my name. I turned around. Stan was at the edge of the woods, looking nervously at the ghosts hovering over the water. I was relieved to see him in one piece.

"Are you okay?" he called.

I nodded and waved him into the woods, afraid of what the White Lady might do if she saw him. Then I turned back to see what was happening to Jeff.

The White Lady was floating back and forth over the water discontentedly. There was no sign of Jeff. *He has to be making some kind of world record for holding his breath,* I mused. The White Lady turned slowly toward shore and started floating up, up, up to the overlook until she drew even with me. The ghost and I looked at each other for a moment. Finally, she nodded to me, her face once again beautiful. Then she beckoned to the dogs, and together they floated out over Durand Lake, growing dimmer and dimmer until they had faded away completely.

I turned back toward Lake Ontario and saw Jeff's head come bursting out of the water. He gasped desperately for air, looking around for the White Lady.

"Jeff!" I shouted. "She's gone!"

I started running down the stairs as Jeff raced from the lake. He looked neither right nor left. He just ran straight up the bank and into the parking lot, leaped into his car, and roared away. I stopped halfway down the steps, my mouth hanging open. *He left me,* I thought blankly. *That no-good rotter left me alone with the ghost and her two dogs.*

It was almost completely dark now. I walked slowly back up the stairs, wondering what to do. Mechanically, I gathered up the remains of the picnic and folded up the blanket. Then I flipped open my cell phone and dialed a familiar number.

"Yes?" Stan answered on the first ring.

"Did you see that?" I demanded into my phone.

"I saw that," Stan said, keeping his voice neutral.

"He left me! He didn't even try to find out if I was all right," I said indignantly. "Would you give me a ride home?"

"I'd be happy to," said Stan. He hesitated a moment and then said, "You know, there's still time to catch a late movie."

I thought about it. On the one hand, there was handsome, popular Jeff who had left me to the mercy of the White Lady. On the other hand, there was my faithful Stan, who had been chased by the White Lady's dogs and had come back to make sure I was all right. Of course, this whole scene might have been an elaborate plot by Stan to get a date with me. Still, the ghosts had *seemed* real.

"Okay," I said into the phone.

There was a stunned pause, and then Stan said, "I'll bring the car to the bottom of the stairs." He hung up.

I could hear his whoop of utter happiness all the way across the park. A moment later, I heard a car engine start, and I knew he was on his way to pick me up. I grabbed the picnic basket and started down the stairs, grinning from ear to ear, to meet Stan.

14

Maid of the Mist

I do not consider myself a coward. I have always faced whatever dangers life threw at me with a brave heart and steady hands. But now my hands were shaking as they gripped the paddle. My canoe was caught in the current and there was no turning back, even had I wished it. And I did not wish it, for life was very bitter to me, and I desired a swift end to my anguish. I had buried my husband before his time, and all that was left within me was a terrible pain that could not be healed. After many days of mourning, I realized I could not go on, and I had decided that death would be better than agony.

But when I heard the distant roaring of the great falls, my hands had begun trembling, and the peace I had felt when I first set foot in my canoe fled. It was, I think, the realization that there would be physical pain before death that made me shiver and shake. I prayed to the Thunderer that my death would be swift and that my courage would remain with me until the end.

I threw my useless paddle away as the canoe entered the rapids and I watched the falls growing nearer, the sky reaching down to touch the very edge of the water as it plunged into the abyss. I gripped the sides of the canoe as the current heaved the small craft to and fro, moving me swiftly to my end. I sang softly to myself, a death song that I had been composing for many days. There was no one to hear me, even if I could sing loudly enough to pierce through the thunder of the falls, but that was no matter.

The turmoil of the water under my canoe increased, but it did not hide the thunder of the cataract. I could feel droplets and soon enough I would see the clouds of mist boiling upward from the abyss. Those clouds would screen my final seconds, and for that I was thankful.

My canoe reached the brink and seemed to hang for an eternal moment at the edge of the chasm. I leapt to my feet with a cry, determined to show bravery at the end in spite of my trembling. And then I was falling, falling through the clouds of mist.

I had expected pain and swift death. Instead, I was caught and held in a strong pair of arms. I looked up through the swirling mist into the face of my rescuer. In his face I saw the wisdom of the ancients, and his eyes, though fierce, were kind. He did not speak, but his voice was all around me, in the roar of the cataract above which we were floating. He was Heno, the Thunderer. He had heard my prayer, and instead of giving me the courage to die, was giving me a second chance to live.

We floated to the great curtain of water, and he shielded me with his body as he stepped through it into the cavern behind the falls. He placed me on a stone bench in the dim twilight behind the falls, and for the first time since I had buried my husband, I broke down and wept out my anguish at his passing and my relief at my rescue.

Heno spoke to me then, and his voice was kind. He told me I could live here with him and his family as long as I wished, until my pain had healed. I thanked him, and he showed me to a room where I could change into dry clothing and rest.

I met his sons when I awoke from the first healing sleep I had had since my husband's death. Even through the anguish I felt at my loss, my heart recognized that the Thunderer's younger son mattered to me in a way that no one else—not even my late husband—had ever mattered. I did not speak of my feelings to him at that time, or in the slow, healing days and weeks that followed. But somehow, he sensed when my heart was ready, and he came to me at that time with soft words of friendship, which swiftly grew into the flames of love.

Heno was pleased by the match, and even better pleased with our son, whom he trained in the ways of the Thunderer. I was as happy now as I had once been sad, and the only thing I missed from my old life was knowledge of my people. Heno sensed my longing, and he would sometimes check on my village and tell me all he had heard and seen of them. And so many seasons passed in peace and prosperity.

Then one day, Heno appeared in the cavern where I was working. I saw at once that the Thunderer, my husband's father, was troubled. When I asked him what was wrong, the Thunderer told me that a great snake had poisoned the waters of my people and that it would soon return to devour the dead until my people were all gone. I was horrified and asked him what I could do to avert this tragedy. Heno told me that I should go back—just for an hour—and warn my people of the danger. I consented at once, and the Thunderer lifted me through the mighty curtain of water and up, over the falls to the gathering place in my village.

MAID OF THE MIST

For a few moments, I stood once more among my people, eagerly seeking out familiar faces as I gave them warning about the evil snake that was causing such pestilence among them. I advised them to move to a higher country until the danger had passed, and they agreed. Then Heno came and lifted me up into his arms and took me home.

It was but a few days later that the giant serpent returned to my village, seeking the bodies of those who had died from the poison it had spread. When the snake realized that the people had deserted the village, it hissed in rage and turned upstream, intent on pursuit.

But Heno had heard the voice of the serpent. He rose up through the mist of the falls and threw a great thunderbolt at the creature, killing it in one mighty blast. The giant body of the creature floated downstream and lodged just above the cataract, creating a large semicircle that deflected huge amounts of water into the falls at the place just above our home. Horrified by this disastrous turn of events, Heno swept in through the falls and did his best to stop the massive influx of water, but it was too late.

Seeing that our home would soon be destroyed, the Thunderer called for me and his sons to come away with him. My husband caught me and our child up in his embrace, and followed Heno through the water of the falls and up into the sky, where the Thunderer made us a new home. From this place, we watch over the people of the earth, while Heno thunders in the clouds as he once thundered in the vapors of the great falls. And still to this day, an echo of the Thunderer's voice can be heard at Niagara Falls.

15

Where's My Liver?

"Go straight to the store and do not fool around," his mother said sternly as she handed over the money. "Your father is bringing home the boss tonight, and it's important that we make a good impression on him so he gives your father a raise."

Tommy nodded, trying to look serious and dependable through the dark mop of overlong hair that fell into his eyes. His father was always after him to get it cut.

"I'm serious, Tommy!" his mother said. "This is important. The boss's favorite meal is liver and onions. I want you to pick up the best liver they've got and bring it home right away. It's a holiday today, and the shops are closing early."

"I will, Ma," Tommy sulked. His mother had really been after him since he brought home a failing report card. Could he help it that the teachers didn't like him? At least the coach had given him good marks in gym.

Tommy stalked out of the kitchen, stuffing the money into the pocket of his pants, and grabbed his bicycle from the garage. He was nearly downtown when his friend Chad caught up with him and coasted his bike alongside. "Come on, Tommy!" Chad called. "The gang's playing baseball over at the park, and we need a pitcher."

Immediately, all thoughts of his errand fled from Tommy's mind. The two boys turned their bikes and headed toward the park. Tommy was hailed as a hero as soon as he arrived and was put up on the mound for the home team. Tommy was good—real good—and pitched a no-hitter to win the game for his team.

By the time the game ended, it was dark. As Chad and Tommy wheeled their bikes out of the park, Tommy remembered his errand. "The liver!" he gasped. "I've got to get to the store!"

Shouting goodbye to Chad, he leapt aboard his bike and rode as fast as he could to the local grocery. It was closed. All the local stores were shut up tight, and Tommy remembered too late that it was a holiday and the shops were scheduled to shut early.

"My mom's going to kill me," he gasped. First the bad report card, and now this! If he lost his father that raise, he would be grounded for life.

He wheeled his way slowly toward home, trying to come up with a plan or at least a good story. And then, as he rode past the cemetery, he got an idea. It was an awful idea, but it would save him from the even more awful fate that awaited him if he came home without a liver. His great-uncle, a retired Great Lakes sailor, had died a few days ago and had been buried in the cemetery. It had been a very cold spring, Tommy reasoned, and his liver was probably still fresh. What harm would it do to remove it? His great-uncle certainly didn't need it anymore.

With the thought came action. Tommy hurried home as silently as he could, slipped in the garage, got his father's shovel, and sharpened his jackknife. Five minutes later, he was back

WHERE'S MY LIVER?

in the dark cemetery digging up his great-uncle's grave. And later that evening, his mother cooked up liver and onions for his father's boss and had actually thanked Tommy for helping her out.

The boss raved about the meal and had such a good time talking with Tommy's parents that he didn't leave until quite late. Tommy heaved a sigh of relief upon his exit and hurried up to his room to change for bed, happy to have gotten away with his ugly prank.

He fell asleep almost as soon as his head hit the pillow and was deep in dreamland when the wind outside the house began thrashing the tops of the trees as if in preparation for a thunderstorm. Yet the sky remained clear, and the moon shone its mysterious light through Tommy's window, casting eerie shadows on the carpet and walls.

"Where's my liver?" a sepulchral voice moaned softly from the street outside the house. "Where's my liver?"

Tommy turned over restlessly in his sleep but did not awaken. Moon shadows flickered across his neck like a noose, and a dark patch on the wall took on the shape of a bloody liver.

"Where's my liver?" a deep voice groaned from the front alcove. "Where's my liver?"

Tommy woke with a start and sat up in bed, sure that he had heard a voice. His pulse started pounding as his eyes frantically searched the shadows in his room. He heard something stirring downstairs, and the sound of heavy feet on the steps.

"Mom?" he called, his throat tight. "Dad? Is that you?"

But he knew it wasn't. He could hear his mother's dainty snore and his father's full-throated blast coming from the master bedroom at the end of the corridor.

"Where's my liver? Who's got my liver?" A ghostly voice rose up from the staircase, deep and guttural. The words ended in a terrible shriek that made Tommy's ragged hair stand on end. He gasped in fear and flung himself under the covers as the thud of heavy footsteps reached the top of the steps.

Thump. Thump. Thump. The footsteps drew nearer, until they reached Tommy's door. "Where's my liver? Who's got my liver?" the horrible voice asked from outside Tommy's closed door.

"Go away. Go away. Go away," Tommy whispered repeatedly, not daring to peek out from under his covers. A bright light was growing in his room, piercing the cotton covers and making his eyes water. His whole body trembled in terror as once more the voice asked, "Where's my liver? Who's got my liver?"

Sheer terror made him suddenly bold. Tommy threw back the covers and found the shriveled white face of his great-uncle right above him. "We ate your liver!" he shouted.

"I know you did, Tommy," the rotting corpse of his great-uncle said softly, stretching out his bony hands toward the boy's shaking body. Tommy screamed.

The next morning, Tommy's parents discovered their teenage son lying dead on top of his bed, a look of sheer horror upon his stricken face. His liver had been ripped right out of his body, but the autopsy proved that the boy had already died of fright before his liver was removed.

PART TWO

Powers of Darkness and Light

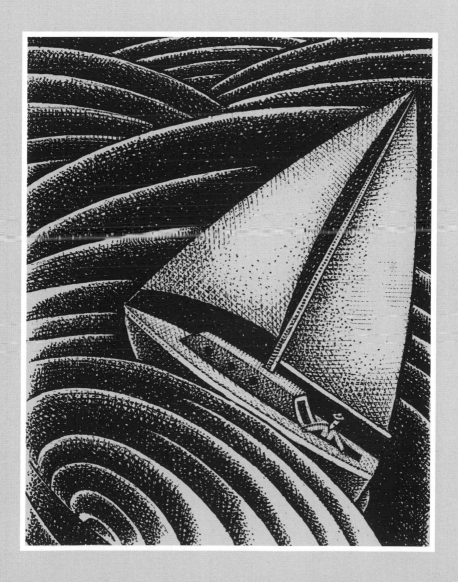

16

A Strange Encounter

THUNDER BAY, ONTARIO

Growing up on the outskirts of Thunder Bay, I was surrounded by stories of the paranormal. One of our neighbors claimed he scared Bigfoot away from his property one night by shooting his rifle three times in the air. He dragged me and my sister to the edge of the creek to show us the footprints. Another neighbor made a hobby of UFO watching. He often talked about the "Day Time Stopped" and hauled out an old watch that had ceased working after a UFO passed over his car.

School was the same. Stories of ghosts and cryptids were common and got worse around Halloween, when everyone wanted to go up to Trowbridge Falls or one of the other haunted locations to scare themselves silly.

I'll be honest. The only cryptids or ghosts I'd ever encountered were in a movie theater or streamed to my TV. But it was fun to hear the stories, and my sister was a firm believer in the supernatural. She had her own hair-raising tale about "the Undertaker," a ghost that shook the back of her car and peered in the windshield one night when she and her boyfriend were parking near the campground.

I was too busy competing on the track-and-field team, both in high school and university, to bother much with supernatural happenings—even at Trowbridge Falls, where my all-time favorite running trail was located. It was not too long, but it had just enough steep hills to give me a good workout.

One day in early summer, I was having a truly terrible day at work. I finally gave up trying to get things done around three p.m. and went out to get some fresh air and exercise, hoping it would put me right. The weather was perfect for running, not too hot, so I drove to Trowbridge Falls to jog my favorite trail and try to regain my peace of mind. I parked my car in the Kinsmen lot, grabbed my favorite water bottle, and set off across the bridge, using my long-distance pace. The trail was surprisingly empty, but I didn't mind the solitude. It had been one darn thing after another at work, and I was peopled out. I preferred the company of squirrels, deer, and one rather droll raccoon.

I was in that wonderfully focused place where it's just you and the trail when I became aware of someone coming through the woods at a fast pace. I heard the thud of heavy footsteps, and realized the person was on an intercept course with me. That was . . . strange. I wondered if I should turn around to avoid an encounter. Before I could decide, I caught a glimpse of a tall running figure in a gorilla costume through a gap in the trees. At the same time, a rather unpleasant scent of sweat mixed with dirt assaulted my nostrils.

Wait! What?!? My brain struggled to identify what my eyes had just seen as my feet carried me automatically along the trail. And then there was no need for recall, because a tall, smelly, hairy individual with a flattish nose, long arms, and very large feet was jogging on the trail beside me. The Sasquatch had an alarmed look on his apelike countenance, which probably echoed my own.

As we ran side by side up the steep slope, I was struck by a crazy notion. Did the Sasquatch think I was running away from something big and scary, so it decided to run away from it too? That seemed impossible, but the big creature looked frightened to my (admittedly uneducated) eye.

It was probably sheer terror addling my brain, but I suddenly wanted to laugh. My new jogging partner was alarmed because it thought I was alarmed. It was ludicrous. On the plus side, the Sasquatch wasn't threatening me in any way, so I decided to keep jogging and see what happened next.

About halfway up the hill, it dawned on the Sasquatch that I was running for sport and not out of fear. He gave me a look of pure disgust and faded suddenly into the trees beside the trail. I managed to jog another 10 meters to the top of the hill before my wobbly legs gave way and I flopped to the ground, right in the center of the trail. My favorite water bottle tumbled down the hill and vanished somewhere in the bushes, but at the moment I couldn't care less. I gave an almighty gasp of adrenaline-laced fear, rolled over on my back, and gazed up at the tree foliage. My heart was pounding so hard I thought maybe I was having a heart attack. What had just happened?!?

As I lay gasping like a beached fish, a long shadow fell across my face. Oh, good lord! He was back. I'd scared the Sasquatch. Again. He was creeping cautiously toward me to see if I was all right.

"I'm fine," I said, looking upside down at the tall hairy figure hovering above my head. "Just winded."

A STRANGE ENCOUNTER

A pair of golden-brown eyes studied me closely for a moment. Then the Sasquatch gave a nod and vanished back into the woods. I heard the birds resume their twittering and knew he was really gone this time.

When I was sure my trembling legs would hold my weight, I rolled to my feet and staggered along the remainder of the trail until I reached the river. I went to the edge of the water and stuck my whole head under. When I stood up, water droplets rolling down my face like tears, I saw a very tall shadow peering at me from behind an evergreen.

"I told you I'm fine," I said crossly. "I do not need a babysitter. It's called jogging. For exercise. Not that you need it." There wasn't any spare flesh on that massive body. The Sasquatch was all height and hair and muscle and long arms. And he needed a dip in the river more than I did. He smelled of sweat and dirty hair—and who knows what else.

The Sasquatch started in surprise. He hadn't realized I'd seen him until I spoke. He made a funny sound, almost like an exclamation, but in a language I didn't quite understand. Then he stepped into the sunlight and laid my lost water bottle on top of a rock. I was touched. Not many people would have gone to such trouble to find it for me. I certainly never expected it from a Sasquatch.

An eyeblink later, he vanished into the woods. That cryptid had some serious camouflage abilities.

"Thank you," I called after him.

I picked up my water bottle and made my way back to the car, wondering if anyone would believe this crazy story. Probably not. Heck, I didn't believe it, and it happened to me.

Then I remembered my parents' paranormal-loving neighbors and my sister's encounter with the Undertaker. I revised that to "some folks wouldn't believe me." Others, well, we'd have to see.

I grinned suddenly. The next time my parent's neighbor talked about the "Day Time Stopped," I would tell him about "the day Bigfoot returned my water bottle." It seemed like a fair exchange.

With a chuckle, I started my car and connected my phone to Bluetooth. I couldn't wait to call my sister. Her head would explode when she heard this story!

Wendigo

ISLE ROYALE NATIONAL PARK, MICHIGAN

His wife was so ill during the autumn that they could not move south with the tribe, lest the journey kill her. So the little family stayed on the island for the winter, gathering as much wood and food as they could to stave off the cold and the dark demons the snow brought with it.

They were comfortable enough at first. Under the care of her mother-in-law and husband, the wife began to regain her strength. But as the winter grew fiercer, the enforced captivity and slowly dwindling food stores lowered the family's spirits, and the wife's newly gained strength drained away.

Finally, there came a mighty blizzard that lasted so long they thought they would perish. After many days the wind and swirling snow died away, and the husband ventured outside. The next storm was already on the horizon, but if food was not found soon, the family would starve. With the memory of his poor wife's thin face and weak form ever before his eyes, the warrior set forth into the white, featureless landscape to check his traps and to hunt for game.

Keeping his knife and spear close, he ventured out upon the most frequently used game trail, watching intently for animal tracks in the newly fallen snow. He saw none, but he stayed alert, watching for movement of any kind, however small. The forest lay still and oddly silent under its gleaming coating of ice and snow as he checked each of his traps. All were empty. Every creature with a shred of sense lay deep within its burrow, sleeping through the terrible winter storms. Still, the warrior hunted, knowing how desperate his family had become.

As he moved through the eerie stillness, broken only by the soft whisper of the wind blowing from the lake, the warrior heard a strange hissing. It seemed to come from everywhere and nowhere at once. He stopped, his heart pounding. Then he saw blood-soaked footprints appearing on the path in front of him, coming straight toward him. He swallowed convulsively and gripped his knife more tightly, knowing that somewhere, watching him, was a Wendigo.

He had learned about the Wendigo at his father's knee. It was a large creature, as tall as a tree, with a lipless mouth and jagged teeth. Its breath was a strange hiss, its footprints full of blood, and it ate any man, woman, or child who ventured into its territory. The poor murder victims were considered the lucky ones. Sometimes the Wendigo chose to possess a person instead, and then the luckless individual became a Wendigo himself, hunting down those he had once loved and feasting upon their flesh.

The warrior knew he would have just one chance to prevail over the Wendigo. After that, he would die. Or . . . he shied away from the thought, too terrible to contemplate.

Cautiously, the warrior backed away from the bloody footprints. The red tracks halted abruptly a few feet from him, leaving him with no inkling of where the Wendigo might be

WENDIGO

hiding, or from where it might attack. He kept listening to the hissing breath of the monster. Was it stronger in one direction?

Gripping his spear tightly in one hand, his knife in the other, the warrior tried in vain to look everywhere at once. Then the snowbank to his left erupted in an icy spray as the creature leapt out at him. The warrior dove to one side, rolling in the snow so that his clothing was covered with the white powder and he became harder to see in the gray twilight of the approaching storm.

The Wendigo whirled its massive frame as the warrior threw his spear. It struck the creature's chest, but the Wendigo shook it off as if it were a toy. The warrior crouched behind a small tree as the creature searched for him. His half-starved body shook with fear. He gripped his knife hard, afraid it would fall from his trembling hand. The warrior knew that he had strength in his famished body for only one more encounter with the monster. If he did not prevail then, he was doomed, and his family with him.

The Wendigo loomed over his hiding place, its sharp eyes spotting his outline against the tree. It bent down, long arms reaching. The warrior leapt forward as if to embrace the creature and thrust his knife up into one enormous black eye. The Wendigo howled in pain as the blade of the knife sliced into its brain cavity. It tried to pull the warrior off its chest with its sharp claws, but the warrior clung to the creature, stabbing it again and again in the eyes, in the head.

Slowly the Wendigo collapsed to the ground, bleeding profusely, almost crushing the warrior beneath its bulk. The warrior pulled himself loose and stared at the creature, which blended in with its white surroundings so well that he would not have seen it save for the blood pouring from its eyes, ears, and scalp. The outline of the creature grew misty and then vanished completely, leaving only a pool of blood to indicate where it had fallen.

Shaken, his heart pounding with fear and fatigue, the warrior picked himself up, cleaned his knife with shaking hands, recovered his spear, and turned for home. There was no time left to hunt for game. The new storm would break at any moment, and he would die if he did not seek shelter. He prayed that what little food they had left would carry them through this next blizzard, though he knew in his heart it could not.

At the edge of the wood, he found himself face-to-face with a red fox. It was a fat old creature, its muzzle lined with gray. The animal stood very still and gazed at him with wise, tired old eyes. The warrior's heart leapt with hope. Here was the food his family needed to survive until spring, brought to him like a gift from the spirits as a reward for killing the evil Wendigo. With a prayer of thanksgiving, the warrior killed the fox and took it home to his starving family. The meat lasted for many days until the final storm had blown itself out and the warrior could hunt safely once more.

18

Black Dog

It was the fall of 1899 when my cousin, who was first mate on a big passenger ship, got back to port from his latest voyage. We had him over for dinner the night after his ship returned, eager to catch up on his adventures. His stories about the passengers always made us laugh.

To our astonishment, my cousin announced during dessert that he was quitting his job.

"Why would you quit your job?" I asked incredulously.

"I met a passenger on our way back to Duluth. The fellow was in quite a state," my cousin reported. "He owns a big house downtown that he split into four apartments, and every one of his tenants moved out. They say the house is haunted."

"Haunted?" my wife said skeptically. "What does that have to do with you quitting your job?"

"I told him about Aunt Kitty. Remember how she used her spiritualist powers to get rid of ghosts for her clients?" my cousin said.

I remembered our spiritualist Aunt Kitty, may she rest in peace, calling on her spirit guides for advice and waving around a lot of incense. And while it was true that she held séances, I didn't recall her banishing any of the ghosts she purportedly spoke with. But I nodded anyway, to keep the conversation moving.

"Well, the fellow got really excited," my cousin said. "He offered me a huge reward if I could get rid of the ghosts in his house. Otherwise, he's going to have to sell it to the city at a loss. They want to tear down the whole block to make warehouses." He named a sum that was more than six months of my current salary. I whistled. That was a lot of cash.

My cousin went on to describe the haunting to us. According to the owner, one day last spring, the tenants heard a strange rapping sound, followed by growls and an unworldly howling sound coming from one of the first-floor apartments. No one was home and the door was locked, but when it was opened, the place had been torn to pieces from top to bottom and the furniture had bite marks as if a giant beast had chewed on it. The police were called, but nobody had a sensible explanation. The tenant had to take lodgings elsewhere.

The police put it down to a sneak thief operating in the area. They evacuated the building and stationed two officers inside to wait for the robber. About midnight, a ferocious growling and howling broke out in the second ground-floor apartment. The quaking officers ran downstairs to investigate. When they kicked the door down, the noise stopped abruptly. When the officers went inside with their lantern, no one was there. But the room was ransacked from top to bottom, just like the first apartment.

Before they could investigate further, they heard a thumping upstairs, followed by growls and a lurid howling that made the skin crawl. The police officers followed the sound from one room to the next, through the whole house. The noise ceased abruptly as soon as they entered each apartment. And every single space was torn to pieces—clothes, shoes, rugs, curtains, furniture, chewed apart as if a giant dog had gone wild.

Within an hour, the entire house was a dilapidated wreck. When the howling came again from the attic, the officers quit the premises. Enough was enough.

"The tenants sent notice to the owner that they were vacating the premises, and the house has been abandoned ever since. From that day onward, folks living in the area regularly have reported sounds of thumping, growling, and strange howls coming from the building, and odd lights flickering off and on, all night long," my cousin concluded. "Eventually, everyone living nearby moved away and the block became an eyesore. That's why the town wants to tear it down to make room for more warehouses," he concluded the tale. "So tonight, after dinner, I'm going ghostbusting. Want to come?"

It sounded kind of interesting, so I said yes.

My cousin hailed a horse-drawn cab, since the haunted house was on the other side of Duluth, and he showed me the contents of his bag as we bowled along the darkened streets. He had the traditional bell, holy book, and candle that were recommended by the spiritualists. He also had some of Aunt Kitty's incense, which she bequeathed to all of us in her will, along with her Ouija board and a notebook, and a pen and ink in case he needed to reach the spirit through automatic writing. I was impressed. My cousin had done his research. This could be the start of a new, very lucrative career.

It was almost midnight when we paid the driver and approached the darkened house. It was halfway down the street, and it looked as if it had been abandoned for several years instead of several months. Broken windows, a sagging porch, weedy yard, and an air of menace that made me back up a pace and take a deep breath. In the light of our lanterns, the blackened windows seemed like eyes glaring at the two of us, daring us to come inside.

My cousin gulped and took out the Bible and the bell. "Here we go," he said, and handed me a large white candle. It took me two tries to light it. I lit a stick of incense too, hoping the spirit of Aunt Kitty would watch over us tonight.

I followed my cousin up the brick path and climbed the steps to the front porch. My cousin held up the Bible like a shield and began intoning the Lord's Prayer, nodding for me to open the front door. "The owner said it's unlocked," he hissed, interrupting his chant. "Go on!"

Heart pounding, I swung the door open and gestured for him to go inside. We entered a long dark hallway full of torn wallpaper and lopsided picture frames. Open doors on our right and left showed two demolished apartments. In the flickering candlelight, I glimpsed torn curtains and shattered furniture. As I stepped forward, my feet stumbled over a man's shoe, chewed to bits.

A large staircase rose at the back of the dusty hallway. As we approached it, a deep growling began. It was such a low sound that it was more felt than heard. My body shook when I heard it, and every hair stood on end.

"Ring the bell," I said urgently. "Ring the bell!"

My cousin kept reciting the Lord's Prayer as he lifted the bell and started ringing it: *Bong! Bong! Bong!*

BLACK DOG

The growling grew louder. The walls around us trembled, raining dust and cobwebs on our heads. At the top of the staircase, a huge pair of glowing red eyes opened and glared down at us.

I frantically waved incense toward the dark shape rising slowly to its feet above us. "The Lord is my shepherd, I shall not want," I gasped, reciting the only psalm I'd memorized. I'm not sure if it was appropriate for ghost busting, but needs must. *Bong! Bong!* My cousin was still ringing the bell.

"Depart, o foul spirit," he shouted. "In the name of the Father and the Son and the—"

He was interrupted by a howl so loud that it nearly burst my eardrums. It rose in pitch until the windows around us shattered.

"Ring the bell," I roared. I dropped the incense and grabbed the bell from my cousin's shaking hand.

Bong! Bong! Bong! Bonga-bonga-bong!

119

"It's not working!" my cousin shouted as a massive paw hit the top step. The wood quaked under its weight. Step. Quake. Step. Quake.

My cousin was staring glassy-eyed up at the creature, Bible and chant forgotten. He seemed paralyzed with horror, and I didn't blame him.

"Yea, though I walk through the valley of the shadow of death, I will fear no evil," I gasped. "For thou art with me." I threw the incense upstairs toward the massive Black Dog descending leisurely down the grand staircase. "And I'm leaving thou, O Lord, to deal with *that*," I added, grabbing my cousin by the arm and dragging him toward the front door.

I dropped my candle on the way out, and a moment later, one of the rotted curtains caught fire. I was chivying my cousin up the front path when the front door shattered behind us and a Black Dog the size of a horse came charging out, barking so deep it made my spine quiver.

We ran for our lives, charging up the deserted midnight street, a massive shadow with glowing red eyes hard on our heels. Behind us, the windows of the haunted house blazed with an orange-red glow as the fire took hold, spreading rapidly through the abandoned rooms.

The Black Dog stopped abruptly at the end of the block, as if jerked back by a leash. It turned on its heels and trotted back to the blazing house, vanishing inside as if the fire did not exist.

The fire department was summoned, and they managed to save the rest of the homes on the block, but the haunted house was destroyed. As the firemen picked through the ruins the next morning, they found the decaying body of a murdered man lying in a trunk in the basement. The man was later identified as a sailor who'd gone missing from his ship last spring. The Black Dog had been guarding the murdered man's grave and had driven away anyone who set foot in the house where its dead master lay. When the sailor was laid to rest in a public graveyard, the Black Dog was seen no more.

While grateful that the ghost was gone, the owner of the house was furious that my cousin and I had burned it down in the process. In the end, the owner and my cousin called it a draw, and no money changed hands. The owner sold the burned lot to the town, which razed the whole block to make room for warehouses, and my cousin gave up ghostbusting and resumed his job as first mate on the passenger liner.

As for me, I started memorizing a lot more Scripture, just to be on the safe side. Who knew what kind of adventure my cousin would drag me into the next time his ship docked in Duluth? I needed to be prepared for anything.

19

The Dark Lord's Curse

DOUGLAS COUNTY, WISCONSIN

It was Johnny Inkslinger, the camp clerk, who first noticed there was a problem. He had just refilled the 20-gallon tank of ink that he drained daily in his effort to keep up with the records for Paul Bunyan's logging camp when he was called away from his desk in the wanigan—that is, the store—to sell about a thousand shirts to the 10,000 new loggers who'd joined the camp for the winter. As soon as he could, Johnny hurried back to his desk. He loved figures (he'd invented accounting and bookkeeping right around the time Paul Bunyan invented logging), and he couldn't bear to be away from his books for more than an hour or so at a time.

Johnny picked up three pens in each hand, nodded to his pet mouse to stand ready to roll across the desk and blot paper as soon as he was finished with each sheet, and prepared to add up the wanigan intake log in one hand while he subtracted the expenses with the other. And that's when he realized that his newly filled tank of ink was empty.

Now, someone other than Johnny might have thought that they'd made a mistake and hadn't really refilled the 20-gallon inkwell before the sudden rush on new shirts, but he didn't make mistakes like that. He had a keen head on his shoulders, which was why he was so good at sums, and he knew without a doubt that he'd just refilled the giant inkwell. He had the stains on his fingers to prove it. So what had happened to all the ink?

Johnny searched the hoses for kinks and found none. Then he looked into the barrel. It was empty. He checked the barrel for leaks. There were none. He concluded that someone was playing a nasty joke on him. But how? The accounting area was always kept locked when he was working at the counter of the wanigan because Johnny wouldn't tolerate anyone touching his ledgers. (Besides, you couldn't be too careful in a logging camp that employed 10,000 lumberjacks.) The only key was the one in Johnny's waistcoat pocket, and it was still in its place. Johnny shook his head. The ink must have been stolen through magic means. There was no other way.

To test his theory, he got ink from the supplies—carefully noting (in pencil) that he was required to use more ink than usual on this particular day—and started pouring the ink into the barrel. It settled in the bottom for a moment. Then a hole magically appeared and the ink started to swirl and drain out of the barrel. As soon as it was gone, the hole disappeared again with a small pop. Ah, ha! Someone had cursed the logging camp's giant inkwell! Johnny got rid of the bedeviled barrel, filled a new one with ink, and went back to his records. But all the rest of the day, he thought about the curse. Was it against him personally, or against the whole camp? he wondered. He decided to investigate.

After carefully putting away his ledgers, and setting a lucky rabbit's foot on top of the new ink barrel, hoping this would discourage more curses, Johnny filled up his pockets with some of his personal lucky charms and sacred relics and made a note to himself to order several hundred more to sell in the camp wanigan (five for a dollar) to anyone else suffering from the curse. Then he went searching for some of the other bosses in the lumber camp. He ran Sourdough Sam down in the giant cooking shanty, which was half a mile long and took about a day to walk around. It was lined with long tables and benches. At one end was a cooking range several acres in length that required three-fourths of the forest to be cut every day just to keep it lit.

Sourdough Sam was hopping on one foot and waving his crutch in the air in annoyance at an under-chef as Johnny Inkslinger approached. Sam had lost his leg in a sourdough explosion shortly after his romance with a witch woman had gone bad, back in the north woods of Michigan last season. He didn't miss it much because it didn't interfere with his ability to cook meals for Paul Bunyan or the other loggers.

"I said 50 bushels of potatoes, not 15!" the cook howled at his underling, who turned red and hurried away to peel another 35 bushels of potatoes for supper. "It's so hard to get good help these days," Sourdough moaned to Johnny.

Johnny nodded sympathetically and then said: "Say, Sam, have you noticed anything strange happening lately in the cooking shanty?"

Sam perked up immediately. "I'll say! The wood doesn't burn as hot as it used to. Sometimes the fire goes out completely, even though a new cord of wood has just been added to it. And the flames near the bottom of the fire—the ones that should be hottest—feel icy cold! Reminds me a bit of that time the witch woman cursed my stove last season." Sam went pale and shuddered suddenly. Clutching Johnny's arm, he said: "You don't think she's come back, do you?"

Johnny shook his head. "She's happily married to an old hermit now and serving him possum stew morning, noon, and night," he reported. Both men made faces at the thought. "But I do think something supernatural is going on around here, and I aim to figure out what it is."

Johnny sold Sam a lucky rabbit's foot for a quarter and told him to put it on the range. "You'll probably need more than one to lift the curse on a half-acre range," he told the cook. "I'm putting in a big order for sacred relics and lucky charms. You may want to reserve a few for the cooking shanty. I have a feeling they're going to go fast."

Sourdough Sam immediately ordered about a hundred more rabbit feet and another 50 lucky pendants, just in case. Satisfied, Johnny continued his wanderings through Paul Bunyan's logging camp, searching for more evidence of a curse.

Johnny was more than 50 feet from the barn when a string of cusswords came bursting forth, blistering the bark of the surrounding trees and melting the snow right out from under his feet. Johnny picked up his pace with a grin. Obviously Brimstone Bill, the camp's boss bullwhacker—what most folks call an animal keeper—was in residence. Brimstone had invented just about every cussword known to man and had written the Skinner's Dictionary, an international bestseller on the best cusswords and torrid terms to use when driving oxen. Bill had dedicated the book to Babe the Blue Ox and his cousin Little Benny, who had inspired him. He'd gone on to write several more instructional books for sailors, bartenders, and other folk who needed to know how to cuss effectively. He was considered the world expert on the subject.

When Johnny entered the barn, he saw a brawny man with a red face and a long white beard wearing a slouch hat, a red flannel shirt, blue jumpers, and big black boots. He was face to snout with Little Benny, who was a rambunctious little ox 10 times bigger than Brimstone, though only half the size of Babe. Little Benny had kicked a huge hole in the wall of his stall and was trying to buck his way out of it. Brimstone had had a ring drilled through the ornery critter's nose as soon as he realized what a rascal Little Benny was, and he was clinging to the ring with both hands, trying to keep the ox from running away.

Brimstone was nearly halfway through his list of 10,000 cusswords, with Little Benny trying hard to toss him through the rafters, when they both caught sight of Johnny Inkslinger. Forgetting their quarrel, they rushed over to greet their friend. Johnny said "howdy" to Brimstone, slipped Benny a couple of apples that he kept in his satchel, and got on with his investigation.

"Strange dad-blamed things going on, you say?" asked Brimstone, toning down his usual cussing on account of Johnny being an educated chap. "We've got a list as long as your dad-blamed arm, don't we, Little Benny?"

The blue ox snorted and stamped in agreement.

"Take a look at Little Benny's gosh-darn hooves, for Pete's sake," said Brimstone, sweating a little because it was so hard not to cuss in front of Johnny. "Them ox shoes keep falling off every ding-dang-dong day."

Johnny bent down to look at the shoes. Yes indeed, they were loose. The one he was studying came off in his hand.

Brimstone Bill let out a string of cusswords that nearly burned off the tips of Johnny's ears.

"Oops! Sorry about that, Johnny," Brimstone said sheepishly. "It's just that Ole Olson put them shoes on only yesterday!"

"He's definitely suffering from a curse," Johnny said, rubbing his burning ears. "An expensive curse, too, if it means making new shoes every day!"

Johnny Inkslinger was becoming annoyed. This curse was costing the camp good money, and he didn't like to see profits going down the drain. He handed a lucky penny to the boss bullwhacker. "You'd better keep this lucky penny tied around Little Benny's neck," said Johnny. "I'm putting in a big order for talismans, amulets, and sacred relics. I'll put you down for a cartload."

"Have you got another lucky penny or two?" asked Brimstone. "Babe's losing his shoes too."

Johnny handed him a second lucky penny and went to visit Ole Olson, the blacksmith. The heat coming from the smithy was nearly as powerful as Brimstone Bill at his worst. There was no snow for almost a hundred feet around the building, and Johnny could see where Ole's footprints had sunk deep into solid rock when he'd carried Babe's heavy shoes to the stable. That had been the first time Ole shoed the big blue ox. After that, Babe had come to the smithy whenever he needed new shoes.

Ole was forging some new chains for the heavy sledges used to haul logs when Johnny arrived. Behind him ticked the massive pocket watch that the King of Sweden had given Paul Bunyan as a gift.

"Howdy, Ole. Watch need repairing again?" asked Johnny. Once a year, Ole took the watch apart, greased up the parts, and made sure everything was in working order. Whenever the watch was taken apart, it made a large labyrinth behind the smithy. The first year it was repaired, several lumberjacks had gotten lost inside the works, and it took Ole three days to find them. After that, Ole set up danger signs all around the watch labyrinth to keep people out.

"'Tis the strangest thing, Yohnny," Ole said in his soft Swedish accent. He laid aside his huge hammer and rubbed his chin in distress. "Ze pocket watch, zhe has always run smoothly, but now zhe need repairing almost every day. Me, I must take her apart to fix, I think. But alas, I cannot do zo right now because there are zo many other repairs to da camp."

"More repairs then usual?" asked Johnny sharply.

"Ya! Many more repairs this season," said Ole glumly. "You know, Yohnny, I think this camp is under a curse."

"I think you are right," said Johnny.

Just then, Sourdough Sam blew the supper horn. Ole closed down the forge, and both men went to the massive dining hall for dinner. On the way, Johnny told Ole all he knew about the curse.

"You vill have to tell the boss, no?" said Ole.

"Yes, it's time to tell the boss," said Johnny Inkslinger.

As Ole took a spot at one of the huge wooden tables, Johnny went over to the massive head table near the half-acre range where Paul Bunyan sat buttering a stack of pancakes that reached nearly as high as the ceiling. Twelve "cookies"— assistant cooks—were running back and forth with new batches of syrup and butter and pancakes trying to keep him fed. Johnny slid into a chair beside him and cleared his throat several times before Paul Bunyan heard him and moved the giant bottle of maple syrup so he could see him. An assistant cook thrust a plate full of flapjacks in front of Johnny Inkslinger.

"How's business in the wanigan?" Bunyan asked jovially as he forked another 10 flapjacks into his mouth.

"Not good, boss," said Johnny, taking a bite out of his stack of pancakes. "Somebody's put a curse on the logging camp, and it's going to cost us a bundle if we don't put a stop to it right away."

"What do you mean, a curse?" asked Bunyan, frowning down at his clerk. Johnny started at the beginning and explained everything he'd seen and heard that afternoon.

Bunyan chewed on the news as he chewed on his flapjacks. "Can't be that witch woman that was hankering after Sourdough last season," he said at last. "She's happily wed to that hermit fellow. Must be someone else. Find out who, Johnny, and I'll put a stop to it. Meantime, we'd better stock up on lucky rabbits' feet and amulets and such."

"Will do, boss," said Johnny, finishing up his flapjacks. "There's one thing I have noticed. Most of the pranks seem to come from down near the ground. The bottom of the barrel, the oxen's feet, the bottom of the fire burning cold."

"Think we've offended some sort of manitou who lives under the forest?"

"I dunno," said Johnny Inkslinger. "I'm going to find out before the camp goes broke."

Johnny marched back to the wanigan and sent a messenger out with an order for a couple thousand amulets, lucky charms, holy relics, and other talismans. The next morning, he rounded

THE DARK LORD'S CURSE

up several of the local tribesmen to find out which of their gods lived in the area and if any of them might be offended by the work of the lumberjacks. Everyone he interviewed was stumped by the situation. The logging camp wasn't violating any sacred ground, and none of the medicine men had any sign that their gods were offended in any way. Johnny was frustrated. How in tarnation was he going to find out who was at the bottom of the trouble?

Meanwhile, strange things kept happening in the camp. One day the cookstove fire would burn so hot that the food would get burned, and the next day they could barely keep the fire going and all the food would be soggy. Barrels and hoops and chains and all sorts of ironwork would rust or crack or get holes and need repairing. Of course, Ole had no time to fix any of them because none of the oxen could keep their shoes on. The lucky amulets helped somewhat, and soon every man in the camp was covered head to toe with lucky rabbits' feet, holy relics, and so many chains that the clatter and chiming they made when they moved drowned out the sound of the saws and the thud of the falling trees.

Some days, the men would get lost on their way to the privy, even though it was only 20 feet from the bunkhouse. Other days, the lumberjacks would spend all morning piling and chaining 50 logs onto a sleigh, only to have the chains snap near the bottom as soon as the last log was loaded. Off the logs would tumble, and the men had to dive out of the way or be crushed to death. Then the men had to collect the scattered logs and pile them on again.

Sometimes the oxen or horses would strain and strain against a load and it wouldn't budge, even when it was sitting on slippery ice. Then it would suddenly come loose and knock the oxen head over heels. By the end of February, only Babe and Little Benny could reliably haul logs down to the river, where they were stacked into rollaways—piles of logs ready to be pushed into the river when it thawed in the spring. Once, all the boards holding the rollaways in place broke at the same moment, and the logs tumbled down onto the frozen river. The men spent a number of hours putting them back into place, and Brimstone Bill was banished to the bunkhouse for fear he would start cussing and melt the river before the men could retrieve all the logs.

Johnny Inkslinger was in a terrible state. The logging camp was losing money to the curse, lumberjacks were quitting left and right, and Paul Bunyan kept shouting: "Johnny, find me the dad-blamed person responsible for this curse!" every night at dinner. The first time he shouted at Johnny, the roof flipped end over end and landed on top of the barn. It took 50 men to fetch it down, and Ole had to make special iron bands to keep it in place when Paul shouted.

"I'm going to have to call in some special help," Johnny told Paul Bunyan glumly as they watched the ice floes slowly breaking up in the river. "I'm going to go visit that witch woman that Sourdough Sam jilted and see if she can divine who put a curse on us. If I don't, we probably won't be able to get our logs to market."

Johnny didn't like leaving the wanigan in the hands of an assistant, but he felt he had no choice. Bunyan couldn't go himself because he was taking the first load of logs downriver to the sawmill. He was afraid something strange might happen on the way because of the curse, and he wanted to oversee the operation himself. Besides, he'd asked Johnny to find out who'd made the curse, so it looked like the task was his. So Johnny loaded the boss up with every charm he had left in the wanigan, and as Paul Bunyan rode the logs south, he traveled east to the home of the witch woman.

A half-day's ride put Johnny into the woods near the witch woman's home. She came eagerly out to greet him and proudly displayed the gnarled little hermit who was her husband. Over possum stew, Johnny told the witch about the troubles the camp had been having all winter. As soon as she ascertained the fact that Johnny was full and didn't want any more stew, the witch poured ink into a saucer and began scrying in search of the person who had cursed the camp.

First she called up several pictures of the logging camp. Johnny saw men felling trees, Brimstone hauling them away on his sleigh, and Ole Olson putting the finishing touches on Paul Bunyan's watch, which was finally fixed.

The pictures in the ink changed to that of Paul Bunyan and his men riding the logs south toward the sawmill. Or were they going south? The witch woman tutted softly to herself. "There's something strange about that river," she told Johnny. "It's been cursed." She waved her hand over the ink, and the picture changed to a bird's-eye view of the landscape. Looking down, Johnny could see that the river was completely round. Paul Bunyan and the men riding the logs were going around and around in a large circle and getting nowhere!

"That's a pretty bad curse," said the witch. "Let's see who made it."

The pictures in the ink started flickering by so fast that they made Johnny dizzy, and he had to look away.

"There he is," the witch woman said at last, and Johnny looked back into the saucer. Sitting deep under the water, in a strange little kingdom of seaweed and sunken ships, was a dark-eyed, dark-skinned manitou god with a long fish tail instead of legs. He had a cruel smile on his face and was watching Paul Bunyan and his men riding in circles in a little mirror propped before his rocky underwater throne.

"Who's that?" he asked the witch.

"That's Matchi-Manitou, Lake Superior's water god," she replied. "No wonder all the curses seemed to affect the bottom of things instead of the top. He must have been sending them up from the bottom of the lake. Matchi-Manitou is a nasty one. Most of the tribesmen hereabouts drop trinkets and other offerings in the water to appease him whenever they travel across the lake. I wonder what happened to make him curse your lumber camp?"

"I have no idea," said Johnny. "But I'd better ride back right away, get Paul off that round river if I can, and see if we can't parlay with the water god."

The witch woman was disappointed. "My husband and I were hoping you'd stay to supper," she said. But Johnny was in a hurry to get back and soon was speeding away on his horse.

Johnny Inkslinger reached camp at the same time as Paul Bunyan and his men finally broke free of the round river. Paul ordered about a hundred lumberjacks to stand beside the river and catch the logs on their next trip around so they could haul them away to another river. Then he strode up to Johnny, his eyes sparkling with rage.

"Who's behind this curse?" he demanded without preamble.

"The Lake Superior water god," said Johnny at once.

"Why?" roared Paul.

"I don't know," said Johnny. "Why don't we ask?"

With a shout of rage that blew over a dozen trees, Paul Bunyan strode north until he reached the edge of the lake. Using his axe like a spoon, he began stirring the lake up until huge waves formed, knocking things around clear to the bottom of the lake. It didn't take long for the dark-eyed water god to appear on the surface of the lake, fish tail thrashing. He rose out of the giant waves, growing larger with each slap of his tail until he was as tall as Paul Bunyan.

"Why do you disturb my lake?" he shouted.

"Why do you curse my lumber camp?" Bunyan shouted back.

"Because you stole my favorite sea serpent and threw him into the ocean," roared Matchi-Manitou. "Bring him back at once, or I will flood your whole camp until each and every one of you drowns."

"Is that what all this fuss is about?" Bunyan asked, calming down at once. "You should have said so. That pesky sea serpent of yours tried to eat Babe the Blue Ox last season. He deserved what he got."

"I want him back," howled the water god, his dark eyes filling with tears like a spoiled little boy. "Bring him back right now."

"I'll bring him back to you if you promise he won't pester Babe anymore," Bunyan said sternly.

Matchi-Manitou promised to keep the sea serpent away from the lumber camp if Paul Bunyan would return him to Lake Superior. He even gave the massive lumberjack a special whistle he used to call the serpent so that it would be easier to retrieve him from the ocean.

Happy now that his pet was to be returned, the water god went back under the lake. Paul Bunyan left Brimstone Bill and Johnny Inkslinger in charge of the lumber camp and went west to the Pacific Ocean to retrieve the sea serpent he'd flung there last season after it attacked Babe the Blue Ox.

Within a month, the sea serpent was back where it belonged, and it was a much humbler and wiser sea serpent after its sojourn in the depths of the Pacific. So the water god removed the curse from the lumber camp, Johnny Inkslinger went back to his ledgers, and Paul Bunyan got all the promised lumber down to the sawmill in time, which made everybody happy.

20

The Dream

The dream, when it came, was so vivid that at first Benjamin did not know that he dreamed. He was making his typical midnight patrol along the stretch of beach known as "shipwreck coast," something he did every night as he executed his duties as a surfman. Ben was one of several men who patrolled the beach each day, trying to prevent shipwrecks and save the lives of crewmen when a wreck did occur.

In his dream, Ben made his way through a screaming northern gale that drenched his skin, tore at his oilskins with whipping fingers of wind, and howled in his ears until it was hard to see or hear anything in the fearsome night. He had not traveled far from the station when he sensed, rather than saw, that he was not alone. Shaking the rain out of his eyes, Ben peered through the roaring darkness and saw a well-dressed man coming toward him out of the furious night. The stranger stopped in front of the surfman and began speaking. Strain his ears though he might, Ben could not hear the man over the massive bellow of the breakers pounding the shore.

Once, twice, three times the man gestured frantically toward the raging lake. He drew close to Ben in a final attempt to communicate, until his face was nearly pressed against that of the lone surfman. Then he vanished without a trace. Ben gasped in disbelief, his pulse pounding harder than the thundering of the waves. Then abruptly, he awoke.

For a long moment Ben lay sweating in terror on the bed and listening to the storm raging outside, convinced that the dream was an omen. Somewhere in the gale there was a ship that was about to sink to the bottom of the lake. But where was it? And when was it going to fail?

Frustrated, Ben pondered what to do. Old-timers claimed there was one shipwreck for every mile along the 40-mile stretch of Lake Superior's "shipwreck coast," and Ben knew that the bones of many a drowned sailor were buried deep beneath the long beach. Slowly, he dressed himself for duty as the surfmen currently on patrol returned to the station, sopping wet but cheerful to report a night free of wrecks.

Soberly, Ben repeated his dream to the crew. They laughed and told him to ignore it. Such dreams were part and parcel of the job, they said. Ben shook his head, but their words helped alleviate the burden he felt. Perhaps they were right. Rigged up, he shoved hard against the windswept door and staggered out into the storm.

Shoulders set against the howling wind and rain, Ben trudged along the 4-mile stretch of beach that was his patrol, stopping at the end to punch the time clock in the key post before turning and walking back again. He strained his eyes over the roaring breakers, searching for any sign of a ship in trouble, but he saw nothing out of the ordinary. Relieved, Ben reported a clear stretch of coast when he returned to the warmth and safety of the service station.

Ben and his fellow surfmen were gathered in the mess for the noon meal the next day when a battered, surf-beaten sailor staggered into the station. The men rushed to his aid, wrapping him in blankets and filling him with hot coffee. When the sailor had recovered a bit, he told his story.

The sailor's name was Harry Steward, and he was the wheelman of the steamer *Western Reserve*. The ship had been cruising for Duluth, Minnesota, the previous day when it rounded Whitefish Point and smacked headlong into the wind. The crew, longtime veterans of the Great Lakes, had kept the ship on course, not an easy task in the growing storm. The ship's owner, Captain Peter Minch, was aboard the *Western Reserve*, taking a trip with his wife and children. Although worried by the storm, Minch had every faith in the men he had chosen to sail his ship, and he managed to keep his young family calm.

Around 9:00 p.m., just 35 miles northeast of Deer Point, the steamer gave a strange heave and shuddered from stem to stern. Then, with a terrible jolt, the ship cracked open across her spar deck just in front of the boiler room. Knowing the *Western Reserve* was going down, the order was given to abandon ship. Twenty-one crewmen and six passengers, including the owner and his family, piled into two yawls and were launched into the raging seas.

The first yawl capsized almost immediately, throwing her passengers into the chilly water. Harry Steward was the sole survivor from the first yawl. He managed to swim to the other boat, which held the *Western Reserve*'s owner Peter Minch and his family, and he was pulled to safety by the remaining crew. They rowed away from the sinking ship as quickly as they could to avoid being pulled down in her wake. A few moments later,

THE DREAM

the *Western Reserve* sank without a trace beneath the waves, a mere 10 minutes after she had cracked from the pressure of the storm.

For the next 10 hours, the surviving crew members kept the bow of the yawl headed into the mountainous, boiling seas and bailed for dear life. Then, a mere mile off the beach, a massive series of breakers capsized the yawl. Once again, Steward found himself thrown into the roaring surf, fighting desperately to stay alive and afloat.

Through the howling storm, Steward could hear the wails of the children, the screams of the women, and the horrible moaning of the other crewmen. But the waves swept him relentlessly forward, and he had no way to reach any of the survivors. Slowly, the voices died away.

Steward, resigned to his own death, nonetheless continued to battle his way shoreward for the next two hours, finally tearing himself from the raging breakers of Lake Superior to collapse on the beach. Sooner than he wished, he pushed himself upright, calling upon previously unknown sources of strength to complete his journey to the life station to summon help, hoping against hope that others, like himself, had survived the wreck.

Upon hearing of the wreck, the keeper had immediately alerted the other life stations, and soon surfmen were swarming the beaches, searching for survivors. Ben was at the front of his sweep, his heart wrenched by the sailor's tale. Of course, there was nothing the surfman could have done to prevent the wreck; it had happened too far out on the lake. Still, he felt guilty, as if it were his dream that had caused the shipwreck to happen.

After a time, Ben stumbled upon the drowned body of a man, face down and partially buried by the sand. When Ben turned the body over, he saw the face of the well-dressed man from his nightmare. Ben dropped to his knees, gasping for breath as he realized that his dream *had* foretold the shipwreck. But who was the man? Reluctantly, he forced himself to search the dead body, seeking the man's identity. Finding a pocket watch, Ben opened it and read the inscription. It belonged to Captain Peter Minch, owner of the *Western Reserve*.

21

The Talking Head

SAULT STE. MARIE, ONTARIO

There once lived a hunter who was so devoted to his trade that he was almost never home with his wife and two sons. The hunter had not chosen wisely when he took a wife, and his head was so full of the chase and the kill that he did not notice that she was fretful and nagging and completely unfaithful to him. All day long, the wife would talk, talk, talk to her sons and yak, yak, yak with the neighbors and nag, nag, nag at her husband when he came home for a precious few minutes at the end of the hunt.

The unfaithful wife had a series of male "friends" who came to visit her at the lodge, and she instructed her young boys never to speak of these men to their father. At first, the boys were too little to understand what was going on. But as they grew older, they became both horrified and embarrassed by their mother's outrageous behavior.

"I am tired of her talking and nagging and complaining," the elder boy said to his brother. "I am going to speak to Father about her behavior." And his younger brother agreed.

That night when the hunter came home, his eldest boy took him aside while the unfaithful wife was outside talking loudly

143

with their neighbor and told him the whole story. When the wife returned to the lodge, her nagging voice preceding her by several yards, the hunter confronted her in righteous indignation and struck her dead where she stood.

And that was the end of that. The boy's paternal aunt came to live with them, and things at the lodge became peaceful for about a fortnight. Then their mother returned. Her voice woke the hunter and his boys in the middle of the night. Even before the mother's spirit materialized, they could hear her talk, talk, talking away as fast as she could. Moments later, she was standing at the center of the lodge, shaking her head at the pretty young aunt who was caring for her sons.

The aunt trembled near the door as the glowing figure of the wife began to nag, nag, nag about the cleanliness of the lodge, the shoddy way she dressed the boys, the shameful condition of the blankets and dishes. The ghost went on and on until the hunter was forced to leave the lodge just to get enough sleep to hunt on the morrow. The boys and their aunt were not so lucky had to endure the ghostly mother's presence until the spirit grew bored and went to visit the neighbor's lodge.

Each night, the spirit of the mother returned to talk, talk, talk to her sons and yak, yak, yak with the neighbors and nag, nag, nag at her husband and his young sister. It was hard to believe, but she was actually worse in death than she had been in life, and she became a source of intense irritation to the whole village. Nothing the hunter tried could rid his lodge of her incessantly prattling presence. Even the local medicine man gave up after unsuccessfully attempting to exorcise their village of her tiresome spirit.

Finally, everyone in the village packed up their belongings and left. The medicine man nicely but firmly told the hunter and his boys to move somewhere far away from the tribe and to take the spirit with them. The pretty young aunt patted each of them on the hand and then departed with the medicine man, who had decided a virtuous woman that could put up for so long with such a tiresome spirit was good material for a wife.

The hunter and his sons went south, hoping to leave the unwelcome spirit of the yakkety-yakking mother far behind. After traveling for many hours, the hunter left the boys to rest beside a large waterfall while he tracked down some game for their evening meal. The boys stood watching the flight of a beautiful crane that was riding on the surface of the whirling, eddying water at the bottom of the falls. Suddenly, they heard a thump, thump, thumping noise coming from behind them. They turned and saw the grisly remains of their mother's head rolling toward them, her nag, nag, nagging voice shouting loudly to be heard over the noise of the waterfall.

The younger boy stared in terror at the horrible, decaying head and then shouted down toward the crane: "Grandfather Crane! Grandfather Crane! We are being followed by a terrible monster! Please take us across the falls."

The beautiful crane looked up from its play. Seeing their predicament, it flew up to the boys and landed beside them.

"Cling to my back," it told them, "but do not touch my head." The boys nodded obediently, and the crane took them up on its back and flew them across to the far shore.

The head of the dead mother screamed with outrage and nag, nag, nagged at the crane to take it across to her sons.

THE TALKING HEAD

"Come, Grandfather," the talking head shouted. "Carry me across the waterfall to my poor, lost children!"

Across the river, the boys watched with apprehension as the crane flew to the grisly, rotting head and said, "Cling to my back, but do not touch my head." The mother's head promised obedience and bounced up onto the crane's back. But the mother's spirit was as indiscreet in life as it had been in death. It was curious to know why the crane did not want its head touched. When they were about halfway across the waterfall, it bumped itself forward and tapped the crane on the head. Immediately, the crane twisted and lurched in distress and the talking head tumbled off its back and fell screaming into the roaring water below.

The head was swept against the sharp rocks, and the rotting brains burst forth from the demolished skull and flew out over the water. The crane banked and flew down toward the battered remains of the mother's head. "You were useless in life," it cried loudly. "You will not be useless in death! Become fish."

Immediately, the floating pieces of brain transformed into fish eggs, which, when hatched, grew into a delicate, flavorful whitefish that became very popular in the region. Thus was the nag, nag, nagging spirit destroyed forever, and the young boys saved from persecution.

When the hunter, upon his return, heard the boys' terrifying tale, he praised the crafty grandfather crane and adopted it as his family totem. The hunter and his sons settled down in the place that became known as Sault Ste. Marie, and their descendants became great hunters and fishermen who ate numerous whitefish and always rejoiced in the flight of the crane.

22

North

DOOR COUNTY, WISCONSIN

In the end, they ran north. It was all they could do. The enemy warriors were pouring into the land with terrible force, killing any who stood in their way. Even killing those who didn't. Death was the only option they gave, and as the stories of their crimes grew, so did the panic. And so the family fled—the warrior and his wife and their three little children. They were not alone. Many others joined them as they ran north. To get away from the invaders was the only thought in the communal mind—away.

They traveled up the peninsula at speed. As they ran, a troubled thought plagued the warrior's mind: What would they do when they reached the top of the peninsula? They could retreat to the island, perhaps. But what if the enemy followed? The enemy always followed.

They ran all day, all night, carrying the children when they grew too tired to run. It was on the third day, as they neared the top of the peninsula, that they heard harsh cries in front of them. Another tribesman, fleeing with his family, had brushed aside a strangely clad, crippled old woman who was hobbling down the path toward them, begging for food.

"Away, old woman. Do not bother us now," shouted the battle-scarred tribesman, snatching his youngest child out of the beggar woman's reach and knocking her to the ground. The warrior sprang forward at once to glare at the bully, war club in hand. "How dare you turn on the aged?" he shouted. "Too soon, we will be old ourselves. Would you have others treat you in the fashion you have treated this old woman today?" For a moment, the two men glared at one another. Then shame claimed the battle-scarred man. He looked away, snapped an order at his worn-out wife, and pulled his family back into a northward run.

The warrior turned and found his lovely wife helping the crooked old woman to her feet. "It is not safe here, mother," she said, her lovely brown eyes filled with compassion. "The enemy comes, hard on our heels. You must flee with us. Our children have no grandmother, and it would please us if you would consent to fill that role in our family." The warrior beamed with pride. His bride, the joy of his heart. The children had surrounded the old woman, patting her arms and back, calling her grandmother. There were tears in the crippled woman's eyes as she consented to join them. "You will not regret your kindness to me," she told the warrior and his wife.

They slowed their pace a little to accommodate her hobble and fed her from their dwindling supplies. There would be time later, when they reached the island, to hunt and fish. Now they must run. Finally, the warrior swept up the old woman's frail frame into his strong arms and ran on, carrying her and his youngest child while his wife helped the older children along.

The shores of the passage were crowded with fleeing families. There were no canoes to spare, and none who had already reached the relative safety of the island wished to make the journey back to the peninsula.

"Do not fear. I will make us a canoe," the warrior told his family with sinking heart. Too long. It would take too long. The reports told of the enemy only a day away.

"We could float across on logs," his wife said, eyeing the old woman and children dubiously.

It was then that the crooked old crone proved her worth. "No need, daughter," she said. "I have a canoe hidden not far from this place. Come."

Taking the two older children by the hand, she led them along the shore until they reached a place where the trees grew right up to water's edge. There she showed them a hidden cache full of dried meat, blankets, medicinal herbs, and a canoe just large enough for one family. The warrior's wife embraced the crippled old lady in joyful thanks for their rescue. Within a very few minutes, they were inside the canoe and navigating the tricky passageway between the peninsula and the island refuge.

They were welcomed by the warrior's cousin and many other members of their tribe who had made the difficult journey north. They set up temporary housekeeping in a clearing with two other families. The warrior immediately joined the men, who were making weapons for the invasion that would surely be upon them in just a few days. They worked as men without hope, knowing that the enemy was far stronger than they and that in the end, their efforts would make no difference. But they would die bravely—all of them. Even the women and children would fight in the end, rather than submit to the brutal murderers who pursued them.

NORTH

Within two days, the north shore of the peninsula was lined with the camp of the enemy. Many were the warriors standing on the banks; many were the canoes that lined the shore. They could hear the sound of distant chanting, see figures dancing ecstatically around the war fires that night. Battle would come in the morning. Death would come in the morning.

The warrior spent that night with his family. None of them slept. They huddled together for the last time, holding each other and listening to the war chant floating over the passage. Just before dawn, the warrior gave each of his children and his wife the knives he had been saving for such a moment as this. Better to die fighting was the unspoken message he sent them as he ceremoniously handed out the weapons. He hesitated when he reached the old grandmother, already a dear member of the family. He had no knife for her. She had not been with the family at the time he crafted the weapons.

"I need no weapon, my son," the old lady said with a smile. She rose to her feet, and she seemed taller, straighter than she had before. Her face looked younger. She pulled his face down, kissed his forehead. Then she kissed each one of the children and hugged his wife, murmuring a blessing upon her.

"Come, my son," she said, and beckoned the warrior out into the dim light of predawn. Baffled by her sudden transformation, the warrior followed. With each step she took, the woman grew straighter, taller, younger, and more beautiful. One by one, they were joined by the other men as they took leave of their families and headed to the shore, there to intercept and fight off the invaders as long as they could. Strangely, the warrior was the only one who appeared to notice the woman in their midst. To the other men, she was invisible.

By this time, the chanting had stopped on the far shore, and the warrior knew the enemy was preparing to cross the passage. He stopped at water's edge beside the old grandmother—who now looked as young and lovely as his bride—and she turned to him, saying: "For your kindness to a crippled old woman, I shall call on the power of the dead in this passage to make an end to the enemies who plague you."

Across the water, the first of the enemy canoes launched into the passage. Behind him, the warrior felt the men tense, heard the sharp, indrawn breaths. Out of the corner of his eye, he saw war clubs raised, arrows notched, spears flourished. But his gaze was fixed on the woman whom he called grandmother as she raised her arms and began to chant in a language he had never heard, her body growing translucent and filling with light.

Oblivious to her presence, the grim-faced men of his tribe prepared for battle. As the enemy canoes reached the halfway mark between peninsula and island, a breeze sprang up out of nowhere, lashing the trees. Out in the passage, the water grew choppy. The enemy canoes were tossed about. And then the water began to swirl at the center, slowly at first, almost unnoticeably, and then faster, harder, and deeper. A giant whirlpool opened in the center of the passage, sweeping the enemy canoes into its depths. The men on the island shouted in surprise, but their voices were lost in the screams and wails of terror as more and more of the enemy canoes were caught in the inexorable grip of the whirlpool. Around and around they were swept, reaching lower and lower, down to the bubbling maelstrom at the center. Those of the enemy still on the shore dropped their weapons and fled in terror at the sight.

It could have been moments, or hours, that the vortex churned. The warrior never knew how much time had elapsed when suddenly, the whirlpool collapsed in on itself, burying the enemy in its depths, never to rise again. A few broken pieces of canoe bubbled to the surface, the only sign that anyone had tried to cross the passage that morning.

Around him, the men of his tribe gave a great shout of incredulous joy, leaping and dancing and pounding each other on the backs. Others called out their thanks to the spirit that had saved them. The warrior stood still and looked at the spirit woman, who was invisible to all save him.

"This island shall be a place of refuge for the pure in heart," she told the warrior as the last of the glow faded from her body. "When evil forces threaten those living in the North, all who seek the safety of the island will be saved, for the passage is protected by the spirits of the dead. Remember this and take courage."

As she uttered the last word, the woman vanished without a trace. A moment later the warrior was caught in an embrace by his young cousin and pulled back to the makeshift village to celebrate the miracle that had saved the tribe from its enemies. In that moment, the warrior vowed to live on the island all his days under the watchful eye of the spirit who had saved his people. His family would stay in the North.

23

Hélène and the Loup-Garou

Étienne spent much of his early life roaming the Great Lakes as a voyageur—an explorer, that is—and a fur trader, following in the footsteps of the "black robes," the name by which the Jesuit priests were known among the American Indians. He was 35 when he met Isabel at a settlement in Quebec and toppled into love for the first time. After a whirlwind courtship, the two married, and Étienne tried to settle down by taking a job in town. But he was an explorer at heart, and a few years after his daughter Hélène was born, he once again began traveling the Great Lakes, exploring and trading furs.

Isabel—still crazy about her man even after a decade of marriage—finally put her foot down. If he was going to travel, they would travel together as a family. And that was that. From that day on, the family traveled hither and yon, and little Hélène was raised on the road. They would settle at various outposts along the Great Lakes for a year, maybe two, and then her parents would move on to the next rich source of beaver.

When Isabel reached the town of La Baye on the western shores of Michigan, she fell in love with the wild beauty all around her. This, she told Étienne, was where they would build their permanent home. It was the perfect place—right on the bay. If the settlement had more English folk than French, what of it? Here in the wilds of the west, survival was more important than ethnicity.

Hélène was 10 when they settled in La Baye, and for the first time she got some schooling and attended church. She was popular among the other children in the settlement, and the boys were already eyeing her thoughtfully. She had long red curls and blue eyes that turned to stormy gray whenever she was angry. By the time she turned 16, she was the toast of the settlement. Many of the fur traders and voyageurs came courting at the little house that Étienne had built for his family on the edge of town.

Out of the scores of suitors for Hélène's hand arose two bitter rivals—the English fur trader Luke Scarlet, a white-blond, blue-eyed fellow with a large brown mole on his right cheek, and Jean-Pierre, a dark-haired, dark-eyed French-Canadian voyageur. Right from the start, Étienne and Isabel knew that their daughter had fallen for the Frenchman, but she was the high-spirited daughter of a high-spirited father, and she led her beau through a mighty dance before accepting his marriage proposal. Luke was sent away with a pat on the hand and a wistful smile. He took his dismissal like a man—at least outwardly. But inside, jealousy against the successful suitor burned like a brilliant bonfire, and the Englishman began plotting against him even before the marriage vows were taken.

Hélène and Jean-Pierre settled in a log cabin near her parents, and Jean-Pierre joined Étienne in his successful fur-trading business. Together, their company became the most profitable in La Baye, adding yet more burning coals to the fire of Luke Scarlet's hatred.

One night in early autumn, a few months after Hélène's marriage, the Englishman slipped into the woods and called on a hermit woman who was reputed to have dealings with the devil. She quickly produced a contract binding Luke's soul to the devil in exchange for the ability to change into a loup-garou—a werewolf—and Luke signed it gladly.

The witch gave the Englishman a potion to drink that burned through his veins, cramping and stretching his body until he fell on all fours in the shape of a giant white wolf with a brown spot on his muzzle in the exact place where the dark mole sat on Luke's human cheek. A moment later, he pushed himself upward and transformed easily into a man again. When he turned to thank the old woman, he found that witch, cabin, and clearing had all disappeared, leaving him alone in the center of the dark forest. Transforming back into a wolf, Luke ran home, rejoicing in his new senses and the ease with which he had adapted to his new shape. It was hard to think of anything but the glorious smells and the lust for blood when he was a wolf, but as a man, his head was clear, and he carefully made his plan.

One afternoon in late November, while Étienne and Jean-Pierre were out checking the trapline, the dark-eyed young man bashfully told his father-in-law that he and Hélène were expecting a child. The grandfather-to-be lit up like a firecracker, thumping his son-in-law on the back and exclaiming over and over again in delight. Neither of them noticed the large white wolf crouched on top of the ridge until it leapt down upon Jean-Pierre, knocking him to the ground in one terrible, graceful movement. Jean-Pierre's astonished shout was cut off abruptly as the huge white beast with one dark patch on its muzzle ripped out his throat. Étienne, frozen in astonishment, came to his senses and grabbed his gun. The wolf sprang away at once, and Étienne fired a shot after it. By the time he reloaded, it was gone.

Étienne dropped to his knees beside his son-in-law, but Jean-Pierre's eyes were already glazed over, his blood pumping out through the fatal hole where his throat used to be. Moments later, he was dead. Étienne carried the body home, so unmanned by the unexpected attack and death of his beloved son-in-law that tears streamed down his weathered cheeks despite his attempts to stifle them. He took the young man to his own house and sent Isabel over to the log cabin to break the news to Hélène.

Hélène was completely devastated, and it was only concern for her unborn child that prevented her from committing suicide. The whole community was shocked by Jean-Pierre's death. Hunting parties swiftly set out in search of the white wolf with the dark patch on its muzzle. But it was not to be found.

Luke Scarlet took the lead in the wolf hunts and was a tower of strength for Hélène and her family in the first dark days following the death of Jean-Pierre. Slowly, as the winter months passed, Hélène turned more and more to Luke for comfort and help. She had moved back home after her husband's death, but she still went to the log cabin once a month to make sure all was well. Her parents were sure that she would move back into her own home with a new English husband soon after the baby was born.

And so she might have, but one evening, when Luke departed into the lightly falling snow following his daily courting call, Hélène—in the manner of all expectant mothers—found it necessary to slip outside to use the privy. As she maneuvered through the snowflakes, she noticed that Luke's human footprints ended a yard or so away from the house and were replaced by the footprints of a large wolf. She lifted the lantern high and examined them carefully, sure she had made a mistake. But she had not.

All the way to the privy and back, Hélène thought about what she had seen. And her speculations were not pleasant. A lone wolf with white fur and a brown patch on its muzzle had killed her husband. And now her English suitor—with his white-blond hair and the dark mole on his cheek—had seemingly turned into a wolf on his departure from her home. Loup-garou, she thought, her blue eyes turning to a stormy gray that boded ill for her suitor.

Hélène behaved in her normal fashion the next evening when Luke came to call. But she slipped to the window and watched as he departed from her parents' home. A few yards from the house, he transformed into a large white wolf with a dark patch on its muzzle and bounded lightly into the trees in the direction of his home.

"Papa," Hélène said the next morning over breakfast. "I saw the white wolf last night roaming near our house."

Her words brought an instant silence to the table. Isabel's fork hung halfway between her plate and her mouth. Étienne stopped chewing for a moment and then swallowed convulsively.

"The white wolf? Here?" he asked incredulously. "After all this time?"

HÉLÈNE AND THE LOUP-GAROU

"I do not think it is an ordinary wolf, Papa," Hélène said meaningfully, jerking her chin toward the family Bible that sat on a corner table. Étienne's eyes widened as he caught her meaning. Not one of God's creatures, acting out of hunger and instinct, but a shape changer who refused to say Mass and had contracted with the devil.

"A loup-garou then," Étienne said slowly, nodding in agreement. He had wondered himself if this was not so because the creature had appeared so suddenly when it killed Jean-Pierre and had disappeared so thoroughly afterward.

Isabel gasped. "Oh, Hélène! Surely not. Why would a loup-garou kill Jean-Pierre?"

"You mean why would a white loup-garou with a dark patch on its muzzle kill Jean-Pierre?" asked Hélène, emphasizing the creature's description. Understanding dawned on her parents' faces and then hardened immediately into anger.

Étienne fingered his gray-streaked beard thoughtfully. "Do you still have that silver tea set from your grand-mère?" he asked his wife. She nodded, narrowing her eyes in understanding. "I will fetch it at once," she said, putting down her serviette and hurrying away from the table.

Étienne spent the day melting silver and making bullets for his rifle. That evening, he left the house a few minutes before Luke arrived, carrying both his rifle and the shiny new gun that had once belonged to Jean-Pierre. When Luke questioned his absence, the women told him that Étienne had gone out to do some nighttime hunting. They did not tell the Englishman what sort of creature he was hunting, and he did not think to ask.

After spending an hour or so teasing the fair Hélène about possible names for her new child, which he swore would be a son, Luke finally drew on his coat, bade his sweetheart and her mother goodnight, and left the house. Hélène and Isabel stayed beside the warm fire, watching it snap and sizzle in the hearth and listening . . . listening.

Five minutes later, they heard the sharp report of her father's rifle, followed swiftly by a second shot from Jean-Pierre's gun, and then Étienne came back to the house, dragging the corpse of a large white wolf with a brown patch on its cheek.

The next morning, the family took the wolf into town to show all the settlers that the murderous creature had been killed at last. Folks gathered around to see and exclaim over the wolf, and several fur traders offered to buy it from Étienne so that they could sell its lovely white fur. But Étienne refused to sell the wolf, and folks assumed he was going to make a rug out of it for his widowed daughter. Instead, he took it outside of town and buried it deep in the woods.

It wasn't until much later that the townsfolk realized that Luke Scarlet had disappeared. But they never associated his disappearance with the death of the white wolf. Most folks reckoned he'd been turned down again by Hélène and had left town to save face. Étienne's family was content to let them think so.

No one in La Baye ever learned the true story until so many years had passed that all the key characters were long since gone to Glory. It was Hélène's son—named Jean-Pierre, for his father—who finally passed the tale down to his grandchildren, and it is still told to this day.

24

Room for One More

When Daniel came to the city for a job interview with a major import-export company, he elected to spend the night at the home of friends in a nearby suburb rather than stay in a hotel. He hadn't seen his friends in several years, so there was much to talk about. They lingered over dinner and then sat on the deck, watching the stars over Lake Michigan until well after midnight.

By all rights, Daniel should have fallen asleep as soon as his head hit the pillow, but for some reason he tossed and turned and dozed, only to waken with a start. He was nervous, but it had nothing to do with the upcoming interview. What he felt was a much deeper dread, like that of a condemned person awaiting the approaching dawn, when the hangman would come for him.

Finally, Daniel fell into a light sleep and started to dream. He was wide awake and restless in his dream, and his dream-self rose and went outside into the lovely moonlit yard. A light summer breeze rustled the tree leaves above, and he could smell the roses that climbed the trellis on the side of his friends' shed. He was considering a stroll to the nearby lakefront park when bright headlights suddenly appeared in the street in front of

163

the house. It was unusual to see a car on this quiet street after midnight. Daniel moved into the shadows under a big spruce beside the shed to watch it pass.

To his astonishment, a large black hearse drew up and parked in front of his friends' house, completely blocking the driveway. Inside, the hearse was crammed with people. The driver got out and looked directly at the tall spruce tree where Daniel lurked. How had the man known he was there? It seemed impossible for the driver to see him in the darkness. Daniel held his breath as he looked into the man's face. It was a twisted, hideous mask with black-rimmed eyes that glowed red in the darkness.

"Come with us," the driver called to him. "There's room for one more." He gestured toward the back of the hearse. The evil leer on the man's face struck terror into Daniel's heart. He broke into a cold sweat, his heart racing.

"No, thank you," Daniel croaked, his throat suddenly dry. He backed away, his hand fumbling for the door of the shed. His fingers closed over the knob, and he stepped quickly inside, shutting it behind him. Then he peered out the small window and held his breath as the twisted form of the driver waited silently at the side of the road for one minute, then two. Finally, the driver got back into the hearse and drove away. When the gleam of the taillights disappeared into the distance, Daniel gasped for breath, his heart pounding so hard that it hurt. Then he woke from his dream and lay sweating under the covers. The smell of roses filled the room, but their scent no longer delighted him. It reminded him too much of the bouquets he sometimes saw at funeral parlors or adorning gravestones.

His friends commented upon his haggard appearance the next morning, and Daniel told them about his dream. "It seemed

ROOM FOR ONE MORE

so real," he concluded. His friends chuckled and told him that he was just jittery about his upcoming interview. Reluctantly, he agreed with them and shook off the fear.

Daniel arrived in the city a little before noon and made his way to the towering office building where the interview was to take place. He met with several different managers during the course of the next few hours, and his interviews went very well. He was sure that he would get a job offer within the week.

Daniel was humming as he left the office and made his way toward the elevator. Suddenly, the scent of roses wafted through the air; he stopped dead, staring at a vase full of beautiful flowers that was sitting on a small table beside the elevator. The floral arrangement reminded him of the bouquets he had seen placed beside gravestones in his local cemetery.

In front of him, the elevator bell chimed and the doors slid open. The elevator was crammed full of people. Daniel counted eight men and women already in the small interior and hesitated, unsure whether to enter or wait for the next one. For some reason his glance drifted sideways toward the roses. Then a voice from the rear of the elevator called: "Come in. There's room for one more."

Daniel looked up sharply, startled by the words, which echoed those from his nightmare. His eyes met those of a tall man with a twisted, hideous mask of a face who was standing at the back of the elevator. The man's black-rimmed eyes had a faint, red glow where the pupils should be. Daniel recognized the man at once: It was the driver of the hearse from his dream.

"No, thank you," Daniel whispered as the overpowering smell of roses filled his senses.

After a moment, the elevator doors slid shut and it began chiming its way downward. Suddenly there was the metallic twang of a cable snapping, then the roar of an out-of-control elevator as it plunged down the shaft. The screaming of the passengers was cut off abruptly by the sound of a massive crash. There were a few follow-up rumbles, then all the sounds ceased.

For a moment Daniel stood frozen in horror, then he ran for the staircase and raced down the many flights to the ground floor to see if he could help. The lobby was filled with emergency personnel by the time he reached it, but it was obviously too late for the people in the elevator.

Seven bodies were pulled from the wreckage. Daniel kept insisting to the rescuers that he had seen eight people in the elevator just before it crashed, but the body of the hearse driver was never found.

25

The Staircase

GRAND HAVEN, MICHIGAN

It felt as if he had been climbing the staircase forever. First one dragging step and then another, up and up. The stairs were old and crumbling. There was a groove worn in the middle of each one, as if many people had walked this way before.

The light around him was dim—always dim; it was hard to see his surroundings. The air was fresh, and there was the faintest breath of wind against his cheeks. Gray trees and bushes seemed to press in on the staircase from either side. He could make out nothing else save this infernal staircase stretching up and up as far as his eye could see.

He wished that he could remember why he was climbing the stairs—or when he started, or how he got here. If he was honest with himself—something he refrained from doing whenever possible—he even wished he could remember who he was.

He dodged that thought, or tried to, burying himself in the task at hand. Keep climbing. Don't stop. Lift one foot, then the next. Ignore the drag of gravity. Ignore the red-hot thigh muscles and the tension in the lower back. Just climb.

But it didn't help. His unknown identity teased him from the edge of consciousness. And he did not like what he saw, not one bit. Something about this endless climb, this dim light, the oddly fresh air with its hint of foreign spices was forcing him to face honesty for the first time since early childhood. His mind shied away from that honesty, but the staircase wouldn't let him hide from himself. Not anymore.

Climb, he told himself, just climb. But inside his mind, he saw the shining, innocent face he presented to his teachers when he denied all knowledge of why his classmate's arms were so badly bruised she couldn't hold her books. They thought her father must be hitting her, and they made a lot of trouble for that family. No one believed that a little boy could be hurting her, and the girl was too afraid to speak up. Eventually, the family packed their belongings and moved away.

He shied away at the memory of the girl's fear, though it had never bothered him before. In fact, he had secretly gloated over it, wishing he could make his brilliant little sister—whom his parents idolized—look at him with the same fear. He hated her; he hated her and he could not touch her. His parents divorced when he was in the sixth grade, and his mother and sister moved far away. Yet she was the one his father always talked about, boasted about, was proud of.

Climb, he told himself, wiping the sweat from his forehead and pushing the wretched thoughts away. Just climb.

The gray trees loomed around him, and he thought he caught glimpses of his sister's face in their shadows. The wind rustled through the leaves, and he heard his sister's mocking voice in the sound. She had teased him ruthlessly for being so "dumb." For getting average grades. For not being very good at sports.

THE STAIRCASE

He pushed himself, mounting the staircase as fast as he could to avoid the buried memories, keeping his eyes on the grooves in each worn stair. Once he clapped his hands over his ears to shut out his little sister's mocking voice. He was the elder, but she was the better! Her theme song from the moment she could talk.

The wind died down suddenly, and his sister's voice faded. When he dared glance at the gray trees, all he saw was gnarled bark. He slowed his steps, the muscles of his legs screaming in agony. He had to rest. There was no landing in sight, so he sat down on the staircase itself. It felt cool and pleasant to his touch, and his legs trembled with exhaustion as he stretched them. Would this wretched climb never end? he wondered, peering into the dimness surrounding him. Would he never make it to the top?

He drew in a calming breath, and with it came another memory: another face from his unknown past. Another girl stared at him in terror. He leapt abruptly to his feet and started climbing again, thrusting the memory away. Somehow, in this dim light, he saw her terror for what it was, and it no longer gave him pleasure. Quite the reverse. The girl's screams for mercy followed him as he stumbled upward.

The wind rose around him, and now he heard the voices of all his victims, screaming in anger and pleading, pleading, pleading with him to stop. Some prayed. Some wept. He howled aloud himself, running upward with his hands clapped over his ears, trying to blot out the voices. In the gray woods, he now saw the girls and women he had killed, their spirits hovering just above the ground, fingers pointed, eyes judging, mouths open to condemn. Not helpless now. They were coming for him! He had to reach the top of the staircase before they reached him.

His soul writhed within him, and the guilt he had never felt before overwhelmed him all at once. He screamed again and fled upward as fast as his legs could carry him, his body slumped almost in half as he tried to bear the horrible pain radiating out from his gut, from his chest, from his mind.

The stairs above his head seemed brighter suddenly, and his heart thundered with hope. It was the top of the staircase. He was almost out of this terrible place. Almost out!

Above him, radiant light suddenly burst forth as if someone had opened a door, and he slowed on the steps and then stopped. The light swirled and pulsed like a living thing, and in its brilliance he suddenly saw himself clearly for the very first time. In that blinding moment, he knew himself as others knew him, and he wanted to die. He was a perverted, filthy, worthless creature with no goodness anywhere in his being. He tried to scream, but nothing came out of his throat.

And then he saw her, his little sister, descending the staircase toward him. She appeared as she had when he last saw her alive, her body broken and bleeding, her face bruised beyond recognition. He had triumphed at her downfall, but now the sight of her made him tremble with agony, with remorse. All the gloating hatred he had felt when he killed her—his final victim— melted away before the look in her eyes as she descended toward him in the gloriously radiant light.

She held out a hand toward him and he backed away, stumbling down the stairs. She said something, but he did not hear her words. He had turned now and was running, running, running back down the staircase, unable to face her.

He deserved her condemnation, deserved every hard thing she had ever said to him in life. But that was not what sent him flying away from her.

In that final moment, he feared something even worse than her condemnation; he feared her forgiveness, and he *could not* live with that. He was her murderer. And not just that. He was a serial killer who had stalked any girl or woman who reminded him of his sister. There could be no forgiveness for him. Not from her. Not from God. Not from anyone. And certainly never from himself.

He ran stooped over, stumbling down a staircase which no longer seemed to go on forever. It seemed short. Too short. He could already see the bottom, and the gaping red-hot doorway rimed with brimstone and fire that awaited him. His victims lined the staircase on either side, standing tall and triumphant as he raced past them toward the door. The very last one in line was his little sister, and their eyes met once just before he stepped through the door.

26

Nishishin Raises the Dead

MACKINAC ISLAND, MICHIGAN

There once was a cantankerous old man who had a fair daughter named Shaningo, which means "beautiful one." Every warrior for miles around dreamed of winning the hand of the maiden, but few dared approach her because of the fearsome reputation of her father.

Now Shaningo was enamored with a handsome young warrior named Nishishin. They had been friends since childhood, and one beautiful summer their friendship was transformed by the glorious fires of love. They wooed in secret, knowing that Shaningo's father would drive Nishishin away just as he had done every other suitor who had approached him. But they were reluctant to run away to be married, for they loved their island home and their people and wished to remain among them.

Now Nishishin was as wise and clever as he was handsome. It was his dream to become a great medicine man as well as a kind and generous husband. After much thought, he came up with a scheme that he knew would accomplish both his goals: to convince Shaningo's father of his worthiness and to persuade the medicine man that he should become his apprentice.

When Shaningo first heard his plan, she was skeptical. It was a good idea, she acknowledged, but would it be enough to bend the will of her fierce father? Still, the only other option was to leave her home and her family, so she agreed to help her beloved carry out his scheme.

The next evening, Nishishin appeared at her home and asked Shaningo's father if he might escort her to the tribal dance scheduled for that night. As predicted, the father was furious that anyone dared to approach his beautiful daughter. He drove Nishishin away with such harsh language and such loud cries that everyone in the village came to see what was wrong.

There were many indignant faces among the villagers when they saw how terribly Shaningo's father behaved toward the young man. But Nishishin faced him with a courage that did not waiver or turn to anger in the face of the abuse. His steadiness won him much favor in the village fathers' eyes. The young man withdrew with dignity, exchanging a prolonged look with Shaningo as he left. This infuriated her father still further, but it endeared him to all those with romantic hearts in the village.

A dispirited Shaningo attended the dance in the company of her father that night. Over the next few days, she grew pale and wan and spent more and more of her time walking along the shores of the lake. Then one night, she did not return to her home. Her father was enraged, sure that the maiden had run away with Nishishin. He woke the whole village with his cries of rage as he ran to the lodge where Nishishin lived with his parents. But to his astonishment, Nishishin emerged from the dwelling by himself. Blinking sleepily, the young man denied any knowledge of Shaningo's disappearance. While her father searched the lodge in vain, the young warrior began pacing worriedly, obviously concerned about the safety of his beloved Shaningo.

The hearts of many were moved by his distress. Shaningo's father was scolded for his behavior and a search party was sent to seek out the maiden. At dawn, her blanket was discovered on the shores of the lake, and a beaded ornament she sometimes wore in her hair was found floating nearby. Nishishin gasped in dismay and wept aloud, sure that his darling had drowned in the lake.

Shaningo's father stood for a very long time holding the blanket in his hands, unable to speak. Then he turned abruptly on the tribe's medicine man and began berating him soundly. The medicine man should have foreseen this! He should have warned the family! Several warriors had to forcibly restrain him and sternly march him back to his wigwam.

Shaningo's father raged for days about her drowning, abusing the elders of his village so fiercely that the chief of the village was finally forced to threatened him with exile or execution if he did not control himself. Meanwhile, Nishishin became almost as pale and wan as his beloved Shaningo had been during the days that her father kept them apart. He spent much of his time by the shore, lighting small fires and praying to the spirits.

One day, two weeks after Shaningo's death, Nishishin appeared before the chief and elders of his tribe. He had been given a message from the spirit world. If he would brave the waters of the lake, swim down to the gods of the netherworld, and plead with them to return the beautiful and virtuous Shaningo, the maiden would be given into his keeping and restored to life as his wife. This he had vowed to do. It was a dangerous

NISHISHIN RAISES THE DEAD

undertaking, but Nishishin felt that life was not worth living without Shaningo beside him, and he was determined to try.

The elders of his village reluctantly gave him permission to go. The whole village—even Shaningo's father—accompanied the young man to the water's edge. After bidding farewell to his weeping mother and grave-faced father, Nishishin leapt into the water and quickly disappeared beneath the surface. He was a strong swimmer, everyone knew, but surely even he could not survive for long deep beneath the waters of the lake.

One minute passed, then two. A few people who had been holding their breath since Nishishin plunged into the cold depths finally gasped, their faces red with strain. Three minutes passed. Then four, and five. Nishishin's mother began to wail softly, sure that her son had drowned. Another five minutes passed. Then 10. Those with a pessimistic nature turned away, shaking their heads at the foolishness of the young warrior who thought he could raise the dead.

Suddenly, Nishishin's mother cried out and pointed toward the water. Someone was swimming up to the surface—no, two people were. A moment later, Nishishin burst through the surface of the water, his arm around the waist of the beautiful maiden Shaningo. The girl was pale and thin, and her eyes had lost some of their sparkle. But she was alive and breathing and clinging to Nishishin as if he were her savior—which perhaps he was.

Shaningo's father gave a loud cry and dropped to his knees. To the surprise of all, tears were streaming down the face of the cantankerous old man. He ran into the water and caught Nishishin and Shaningo in an embrace, squeezing them both until they could barely breathe. Shaningo finally had to scold him, warning him that he was about to send her back to the netherworld from which she had just emerged.

The father pulled the two young people from the water and had them married right there and then on the shore. He could not stop weeping, and he could not say enough good things about Nishishin, his beloved son-in-law who had returned life to his daughter.

From that moment on, whatever Nishishin said was law to Shaningo's father. He built the couple an enormous wigwam right next to his own, furnishing it with the very best of his property, all the while thanking his son-in-law for raising his daughter from the dead with every breath he took.

Nishishin was revered by his people as a holy man, and the tribal medicine man took the young man as his apprentice. Nishishin, happy with his lovely wife, a growing family, and a new profession, never told anyone his secret. But once each year, on the anniversary of her "resurrection," Nishishin and Shaningo would slip out of their wigwam and swim underneath the lake, through a short underwater tunnel and into the large cave that had once sheltered the maiden for two weeks. There they spent a romantic night together, cuddled up around a small fire, eating a special meal that Shaningo had prepared for them and rejoicing in the successful outcome of their plan.

The Wizard's Rope

PORT HURON, MICHIGAN

I'd left my old ship at Port Huron—creative disagreement with the captain—and spent a few weeks living off my earnings and taking in the sights. I'd grown up in this town and had become a sailor as soon as I found a captain who would sign me on as cabin boy. Solid ground makes me nervous. So when I'd finished blowing my money on the usual pursuits—wine, women, and gambling—I signed on with an old-world captain heading to Chicago.

Now old-world captains—top-ranking sailors that migrated to the States from seafaring countries around the globe—have a pretty stern reputation on the Great Lakes. They were real efficient and could pinch a dime until it cried for mercy. The ship owners loved them, but the crew didn't always agree. They were ambitious and worked so hard they often won jobs over the local boys, who consequently resented them. And you couldn't beat them when it came to making a fast run through the lakes from Oswego to Milwaukee. Folks claimed they were wizards who knew how to control the winds and the storms, but I figured that was a lot of hogwash. Sour grapes from some of the mates who thought they'd make captain first, and had been mistaken.

I loved my new ship—she was a brand-new 201-foot-long, three-masted schooner carrying a cargo of iron ore—and I quickly grew to admire her captain. There would be no creative differences here. I'd tow the line like every man jack aboard or get tossed into the frigid waters of the lake. The water was as flat as a pancake, and we made Chicago in record time.

I decided to stick with the ship awhile longer and was back onboard well before sailing time. We were halfway up Lake Michigan when the wind died away altogether, and the ship was becalmed in the middle of nowhere. I was ready with a whistle and a few silver coins in my pocket—a time-honored sailor's practice for calling a wind—but the first mate laid a hand on my arm and told me to wait. I found the mate's order strange until I looked around and saw everyone else waiting too, their eyes fixed on the captain's cabin.

All work had ceased, and tension mounted on the deck, releasing only when our stern captain strolled up on deck in his spankin' new uniform with a knotted rope in his hands and went to the bow of the ship. As we watched, the old man slowly unraveled one of the small knots at the top of the rope. Instantly a breeze sprang up, filling the sails and throwing the crew into a frenzy of work adjusting the ropes and canvas. I watched the captain surreptitiously as I worked and saw him release a few more knots while the wind built up slowly around us. Then we were sailing north and gaining speed with each moment that passed. The captain barked out a few commands and retired to his cabin with the rope.

I was a bit spooked by what I had seen. I thought all that talk about wizards was a lot of hokum, but I had no other explanation for what I had just seen. Our captain had just used an ordinary knotted rope to call the winds.

I asked the first mate about it, privately, when our watch was over. He treated the whole matter quite casually, as if it were quite normal to sail under a "Master of the Winds"—what we call a sailor-wizard.

"You should see the old man when there's a storm brewing," he said with a grin.

I smiled weakly in return, vowing that I would get off this ship as soon as I could. Who knows what a wizard would do to you if you ever crossed him? If the captain could control the winds and the storms, what other things . . . or creatures . . . could he summon out of the depths? I decided to ship off when we reached Port Huron.

We were nearing our destination when a mighty squall rose up out of nowhere. As soon as the mate saw the roiling black clouds on the horizon, he went running for the captain. The storm was coming on fast, and the swells were already rolling the ship from side to side when the captain went forward to the bow with his rope. He jerked two large knots apart fast and a huge wind slammed away from the ship, heading out toward the storm. I saw the wind smash directly into the clouds, driving them backward. For a moment, the storm wind and the captain's wind fought with one another, and the sea beneath them churned and whirled. A waterspout descended from the fighting clouds and I drew in my breath sharply, fearing for my life.

THE WIZARD'S ROPE

At the bow of the ship, the captain released a third large knot near the bottom of the rope, and a second wind raced away toward the storm. When this wind hit the storm clouds, they began to recede, heading toward Canada. Lake Huron was choppy and hard to manage for the next few hours, but the fierce squall had disappeared into the distance and the danger was gone. The first mate gave me a knowing grin as I passed, and I nodded to him. I no longer wondered why the men sailed with an old-world wizard. A man who could chase away a Great Lakes squall with a few twists of his fingers would earn any sailor's loyalty. Right then and there, I changed my mind about leaving.

The captain's wife joined the ship when we sailed out of Buffalo, and I'd never met a sterner, more forbidding woman in my life. Most men would have fled in terror before such a lady, but she seemed to suit the captain. I wondered if she knew that he was a wizard, but I never saw him bring out the rope after she came aboard, so I decided that she did not.

I thought things were strict under our captain, but I saw I was wrong. No one dared step one inch out of line when the wife was onboard. The men doffed their caps when she went by and said "please" and "thank you" in the mess, even when she wasn't present. They even stopped swearing.

I cussed just once after she came aboard, and the lecture I got in manners from that formidable lady rang in my ears for hours. The crew gave me sympathetic smiles all that day. I realized that this sort of thing had happened before to the new man onboard; a kind of sailor's initiation rite.

"You should'a warned me," I complained to the mate, but he just gave me his cheeky grin.

"Best to learn these things for yourself," he said.

"Ha!" I said to his retreating back, but he just hummed merrily under his breath and went to check the rigging.

The captain's wife was appallingly clean. I thought the ship was in good shape when we arrived in Buffalo, but the lady was not pleased. I spent most of my waking hours scrubbing the decks, yet somehow she always found a spot I'd missed.

We sailed across Lake Erie, threaded our way through Lake St. Clare and the St. Clare River, and then were out on Lake Huron and pulling into my home port. By then, I was sorely tempted to abandon ship, since I wasn't sure how much more I could take of the captain's wife. Still, I would probably never find a safer ship in all my born days, and the mate assured me that she took only one trip onboard the ship each year. So I stayed aboard, and a few days later we left Port Huron and set sail up the lake, heading for Chicago.

We were only a few hours out of port when the captain's wife approached his quarters with a broom and a mop. Up until that period, the captain had managed to keep his wife from doing more than a cursory cleanup in his quarters and had forbade her to enter the private alcove where he kept all the ship's records (and, I suspected, his wizardly tools). But the look she gave her husband would have cowed a stronger man than our captain. He retreated with as much dignity as possible and went to inspect the belowdecks.

With the captain and his lady both occupied, things were quite peaceful up on deck. Until the first of the winds arrived, whooshing out of the captain's door and wrapping around us before taking off up into the sky. The ship lurched as the rising winds competed with those currently filling our sails. But there was more to come.

Fierce storm winds shuddered forth from the cabin: whirlwinds and roaring nor'easters. Around me, men were shouting and grabbing onto anything they could hold. Two blokes were swept off their feet and right over the side of the ship as I staggered forward against the hurricane-force wind that was spinning the ship around and around in circles. I managed to catch hold of the door to the captain's quarters. Inside, I saw that woman undoing the last of the knots in the rope, the big one on the bottom.

"No!" I shouted, but it was too late. The knot came undone, and the winds from a thousand gales that had been tied into that knot were released all at one go. The ship exploded under the fierce onslaught, and I felt myself tossed high into the air, both hands still gripping the captain's door. Then something struck me in the head and everything went black.

I came to my senses many hours later, surprised to be alive, and found that I was floating half on and half off the captain's door, held there by the buttons of my jacket, which had become jammed into the hinge. Thank God for those buttons, I thought fervently, knowing that I would have sunk to the bottom of the lake and drowned without them.

There was no sign of my ship, and what debris surrounded me was very small indeed. The waves I was coasting upon were still rough in the aftermath of the windy onslaught, but the sky was crystal clear above me. I dragged myself on top of the door and rode the waves to the shores of Michigan, arriving on a sandy spit much more quickly than I would have expected.

I lay on the beach next to the captain's door until some of my strength returned. Then I hotfooted it for Port Huron, only a few miles south of my landing place. I made my way to the home of my cousin, who took me in and tidied me up. He was pleased to learn the cause of the mysterious windstorm that had swept the coast a few hours before, and he agreed that I was lucky to be alive. We decided it would be best if I didn't tell the whole truth about the shipwreck. Folks might get nervous if they found out that there really were "Masters of the Wind" out there.

It took me a month to recover my nerve, but after that I signed on with another ship and was back out on the lakes. You can be sure my captain was born in America. I wasn't taking any chances with old-world captains ever again.

28

The Storm Hag

ERIE, PENNSYLVANIA

"She lurks below the surface of the lake near Presque Isle," his uncle once told him, "her lithe form forever swimming through the weeds and the mire. Pale and green of skin, her yellow eyes shine luminously in the dark, and her thin, long arms wrap themselves around the unwary, while foul-green pointed teeth sink into soft flesh, and sharp nails at the end of long, bony fingers stroke you into the deepest sleep there is."

"What is she?" he had asked, his eyes wide with amazement and fear.

"She is known by many names," his uncle said, "but to sailors of Lake Erie, she is the Storm Hag."

He was only a young boy when his uncle first told him about the Storm Hag. Over the years, his uncle told him more. The creature was a sea witch, his uncle said, an evil Jenny Greenteeth who summoned the storms and pulled shipwrecked sailors down into her evil embrace to live with her forever at the bottom of the lake. Sometimes she would wait until the calm right after the storm to attack. When the sailors relaxed their guard, lulled into thinking that the danger had passed with the storm, the Storm Hag would burst forth from the dark waters of the lake, spewing forth lightning and wind like venom. And the ship would vanish—never to be seen again.

As he grew older, he realized that the Storm Hag was just a fairy tale told to amuse and frighten a little boy. His uncle came from Scotland and told many stories of bogeymen and witches. With the scorn of young adulthood, he discarded all of his uncle's tales and warnings, taking his 24-foot sailboat out into rough seas. He gloried in the unexpected gales that sprang up on Lake Erie and loved to test his seamanship against the storms.

One evening, after a difficult day at work, he decided to take a sail on the lake. There was a small craft warning out, but he was an expert sailor and took no heed. Soon he was in the deep waters, buffeted this way and that by the wind and the waves and enjoying every moment. The sky was darkening into night when he saw the ominous storm clouds gathering together on the horizon. The wind grew damp and chill, and he felt the first twinge of fear. He had sailed far out on the lake, and the storm was coming quickly. Turning his boat, he took down the sail, started the engine, and hurried toward Presque Isle and safety.

The storm caught him halfway home, and it took all his wits and strength to stay afloat. Rain lashed his body, soaking him to the skin and getting into his eyes until he couldn't see. Around him, the wind shrieked and gurgled and howled. Amid the chaos, he though he heard the sound of a voice crooning:

Come into the water, love,
Dance beneath the waves,
Where dwell the bones of sailor lads
Inside my saffron cave.

It was a trick of the storm, he told himself, tightening his grip on the wheel. Then he saw a grotesque but lissome form rise from the waves off the port bow. A catlike green face with a squashed nose, glowing yellow eyes, and long teeth was framed by seaweed-strewn hair that writhed like sea eels. Sharp spikes protruded from the spine, and the body was covered with green scales. In place of legs, the figure had a long fish tail. It was the Storm Hag. Her arms stretched longingly toward him through the raging storm, and she beckoned to him with bony fingers.

"Come into the water, love," she crooned. "Dance beneath the waves."

"Get out of here," he shouted desperately. "Leave me alone!"

She swam closer, and he turned the wheel as hard as he could in alarm. A giant wave broadsided him, nearly tipping the boat. He fought fiercely with the recalcitrant wheel and finally regained control. The Storm Hag laughed at his dilemma and started singing again: "Come into the water, love, / Dance beneath the waves."

She was keeping pace with the boat, and he knew that the evil creature was toying with him. Heart pounding with fear, he grabbed a bait bucket and hurled it through the howling wind and rain toward the Storm Hag. The bucket hit the creature in the head, knocking her backward for a moment. She gave a shriek of anger and pain, clapping a clawed hand to her injured head. Then she disappeared beneath the pounding waves.

With a shout of triumph, he gunned the motor and turned the boat for Presque Isle and safety. He was almost within hailing distance of the island when the storm ceased as abruptly as it had started. The rain and wind died away to nothing, and

THE STORM HAG

the waves began to calm down to a more manageable level. He glanced around fearfully, but there was no sign of the Storm Hag, and he knew that he had won through to safety. Thank God for bait buckets, he thought fervently.

At that moment, the boat gave a strange lurch and began moving backward. The wheel twitched under his hands and then spun around and around, out of control. He tried to grab it, but it was moving so fast it nearly broke his arms, and he let go. He glanced around fearfully, and realized that his boat was caught up in a massive whirlpool that had sprung up just off the island. Around and around his boat swirled, floating backward into an ever smaller circle while a strange wind blew around him, small waves splashed over the bow, and droplets of mist clouded his eyes.

From the bottom of the whirlpool, a sweet voice began to croon:

Come into the water, love,
Dance beneath the waves,
Where dwell the bones of sailor lads
Inside my saffron cave.

He gave a shriek of terror as he realized that he was once again in the clutches of the Storm Hag. And then he saw her, rising out of the swirling whirlpool, her arms outstretched toward him.

"Come into the water, love," she shouted, wrapping her arms around him. He uttered one cry of sheer horror as her foul-green pointed teeth sank into the soft flesh of his face, and her sharp nails stroked down his back, tearing the skin away from his bones.

Moments later, the whirlpool was gone, and there was only the harsh beating of storm waves against the island that lessened as the wind died away to nothing. The boat and its young owner vanished without a trace, and only his uncle ever suspected the truth behind the disappearance.

29

I Must Get Home

BUFFALO, NEW YORK

The woman contacted the brig's captain unexpectedly, requesting a special late-season charter to take her to Chicago. "I must get home," she told him, "no matter the price." There was quite a lot of money involved, and as a bonus, the captain had found a shipment of spirits to sell in Chicago. So he accepted the charter and told the first mate to round up an impromptu crew—not an easy feat at the end of the season.

The first mate caught a flash of the rich passenger's lovely face beneath a fashionable veil as she boarded the ship in Buffalo. "She's pale as death," he whispered to himself, touching the brim of his cap before turning away to supervise the loading of the barrels into the hold of the brig.

He soon forgot the pale lady as a tug towed them to the mouth of the harbor and they set sail westward. They were sailing with a limited crew—just the captain, himself, the cook, and five men forward. None of the men were part of the regular ship's complement, so the mate watched closely to make sure they did their jobs correctly.

A strong northeast breeze blew up and kept them sailing well, though the lake grew choppy in the morning. The rich passenger did not appear all day—a fact the first mate attributed to seasickness. The cook had rapped on her door with an offering of tea and biscuits, but had received no answer.

They made good time across Lake Erie, arriving near Colchester Reef at dusk the second day. There was still no sign of the pale lady, though the lake was smooth and the bright sun had made the day's sail a pleasure. The first mate wondered why she stayed belowdecks, but work kept him too busy to ponder, for the ship was entering the dangerous waters leading up to the Detroit River.

Suddenly the first mate was almost thrown overboard by the violent rolling of the ship. Cursing, he rushed over to find the wheelman in a daze from a high fever. The sailor was rocking unsteadily, so the first mate grabbed the wheel to steady the ship. He ordered the ailing man belowdecks, where he was placed in isolation to prevent the spread of the disease.

Just before dawn, a tugboat stopped alongside the brig to give them a hawser for the tow up the river. When the first mate came topside to take the next watch, he saw the pale lady standing beside the rail, watching the tugboat. Her figure almost glowed in the light of the setting moon. She looked like a ghost.

The first mate turned away with a shudder, thinking it was a bad omen. He hurried over to speak with the captain, who told him a second crewman had fallen ill with fever during the night watch. They had taken the man belowdecks and the captain had given him some medicine from their supply box.

Overhearing the conversation, the pale passenger murmured, "Poor man. Poor man. But I must get home, no matter the price."

The first mate was grim as he took command of the watch. Two men sick already—what an ill-fated journey!

The ship dropped the towline at dusk and continued onto Lake Huron under a steady breeze. The first mate thanked his lucky stars that the weather had remained fine. He did not relish the notion of being shorthanded during a lake hurricane.

The next morning, the cook fell ill with the same high fever that had struck the two crewmen. The captain ordered him to bed, and the sailors had to make do with their own meager cooking skills. There was no sign of the pale lady during the day, and no response when the first mate knocked on her door to ask if she would like some stew.

At dusk the captain retired belowdecks for a short break but failed to return topside. With a sinking heart, the mate went down and found the captain in his bunk, tossing and turning with fever. The first mate doused him with a tonic from their rapidly depleting medical supply and sent one of the healthy crewmembers to sit with him.

Assuming temporary command of the ship, the first mate remained on deck that evening. The pale lady materialized around midnight, and the first mate realized that she appeared healthier than before. The closer she got to Chicago, the better she seemed to feel. But her renewed vigor had come at a great cost, for the former wheelman and the cook had died earlier that night. The sailors had wrapped up the bodies and placed them in the hold.

"Poor men," whispered the pale passenger. "Poor men. But I must get home, no matter the price."

They headed into the Straits and came abeam of Old Mission Light near dawn, just as another crewmember was stricken with

I MUST GET HOME

the same fever that had killed the cook and the wheelman. With only two healthy men and himself to keep the ship on course for Chicago, the mate grimly considered his options. It was difficult but not impossible to reach their destination, but only if the weather remained fair. Given their current location, there was no good place to dock, even if he had wished it. He decided to stay the course as long as possible, though he could no longer spare a man to cook for the passenger nor to watch over the sick.

The storm struck suddenly, with no warning. One moment there was a clear blue sky; the next, the brig was rocking violently in the waves. One after another, the sails were ripped off the masts. The ship rolled and pitched, but with the poles bared, the mate and his two remaining crewmen managed to get her back under control. When the ship was stabilized, the mate left both hands manning the wheel and slipped below the gyrating deck to secure the safety of the sick, the passenger, and the captain.

The first mate knocked loudly on the passenger's door but there was no response. Alarmed by the silence, he thrust the door open, afraid the pale lady had been injured, but he found the room empty. He returned to the rocking passageway and carefully made his way to the captain's cabin. Thrusting it open, the mate saw the captain lying dead on his bed. The pale lady leaned over him with sorrowful eyes.

"Poor man, poor man," she whispered. "But I must get home, no matter the price."

The passenger was glowing in the dim light of the cabin, and the first mate realized that he could see the captain's bunk right through her translucent body. The pale lady was a ghost!

With a shout of horror, the mate leapt backward into the passage and ran up the ramp to the quarterdeck. Topside, he saw that the wheel had been smashed and the two crewmen swept overboard. Lightning flashed, thunder rumbled, and the downpour drenched him as the mate staggered forward, his eyes on the massive, straining masts. The ship was rolling terribly in the waves, and the first mate knew they were all doomed. Their fate had been sealed the moment a phantom commissioned their captain to take her across the Great Lakes to Chicago.

The ship rocked wildly, and the first mate fell to the deck against the mainmast fife rail. He rolled over and looked up in horror as the pale woman materialized suddenly. The phantom floated directly above him in the dim light of the storm and screamed: "I must get home, no matter the price."

Then the ship capsized, throwing the mate into the chilly waters of the lake. Surfacing almost immediately, he grabbed hold of a floating grate and hung on while the ship slid below the surface. He was still drifting hours later when the storm abated. He was nearly dead from cold and exhaustion when he was found by a fisherman and taken in.

When he had recovered enough to tell his tale, the mate reported a sudden storm that capsized his ship. He made no mention of the high fever that had stricken the crew or the pale ghost that doomed them. Who would believe him?

The wreck went unremarked and unlamented, for which the mate was glad. No one in Chicago had any interest in the ship, which was uninsured and had belonged solely to her dead captain. The makeshift crew had been composed of drifters who had no families to speak of.

When he returned to Buffalo, the mate made a few cautious inquiries about the ghost. A retired sailor told him the story of a rich bride who moved to Buffalo with her indifferent husband more than a century ago. She longed for her family back in Chicago, so one autumn she commissioned a ship to take her home for a visit. It was dangerous to sail the Great Lakes so late in the fall, but the woman had insisted, saying: "I must get home, no matter the price." But the ship sank during a sudden storm, and the woman and all hands aboard were lost.

"The pale lady has been trying to get home ever since," the old sailor said sadly. "More than one captain has been fooled into taking the phantom aboard, and every time, the ship goes down somewhere in Lake Michigan."

The mate thanked the retired sailor for the tale and went home to pack his belongings. For some unknown reason, the pale lady had spared his life, and he was not going to waste it. His father wanted him to take a position in the family firm, and that's just what he was going to do. He was done sailing the Great Lakes.

30

Resurrectionists

It was the fall of 1884 when the three of us old friends met for a drink at the local pub. We were boyhood pals, and we tried to get together whenever all three of us were in Kingston. Chester had just moved to town and had applied for a job at the newspaper. I was working down at the docks and hated my new boss, who found fault with everything I did. And Luke was studying to be a doctor at the local medical school.

When our pints arrived, Luke started complaining about a policy his medical school had. They insisted that students provide their own cadavers to do their studies.

"And they don't tell you where or how to purchase a cadaver either. It's totally unfair," Luke said.

After asking around, Luke finally found a resurrectionist with a body he could purchase for his studies. But he had to pay the man a bundle of money for the body, and no questions asked.

"It cost me an arm and a leg," he complained bitterly, utterly failing to see the irony in his statement. "Honestly, I could earn more in one night grave robbing than either of you could earn in a month of honest toil."

His eyes narrowed suddenly. I could almost see the wheels turning in his head. He looked at me, then at Chester, and then smiled. There was greed in that smile. It made me feel uneasy. Luke had always been good at getting me and Chester in trouble when we were kids. And it looked like he was about to do it again.

"We should become resurrectionists," he said.

And there it was.

Chester protested. I protested. But Luke was persuasive. Once a person has passed away, he or she didn't need their body anymore. It said so right in the Good Book. They were getting a new one, come Judgment Day. And we'd be advancing the cause of science. In the end, we both said yes, just as Luke knew we would.

We chose a moonless night for our first adventure. Chester and Luke had been scouting all the churches and graveyards in the vicinity, and I'd been watching the newspapers for funeral announcements. Between us, we came up with a couple of good candidates who'd shuffled off the mortal coil in the last few days. As soon as it got dark, we went to work.

"First up is a man named Jacques Moreau," Chester announced as he slid onto the seat of the wagon and picked up the reins. Soon we were trotting down the road toward a cemetery south of town. We quickly came abreast of a wrought-iron fence that announced the start of the graveyard. Chester cautiously nosed the wagon inside the gates and drove to a corner lot, where the lantern Luke was holding showed a new headstone and recently disturbed earth. Glancing at the headstone, I read: "Sacred to the memory of my husband Jacques. His comely young widow yearns to be comforted."

Chester laughed when he saw the stone and said, "Here you go, Luke. You can spark with the Widow Moreau!"

I shook my head and handed around the shovels. It was slow, hot work digging up a coffin. We shoveled the dirt onto a canvas tarp laid by the grave so that the nearby grounds remained pristine. We started the digging at the head of the grave clear to the coffin. We covered the lid in sacking to muffle noise, and Chester used a crowbar to pull it free. And there was Monsieur Jacques Moreau, resurrected at last, though perhaps not the way he'd been expecting.

The old man was not good to look upon when we pulled him out. Widow Moreau had decked him out in his best suit, but his white hair flopped wildly as we lifted him up, and nothing could improve the collapsed, withered look to his face or the greenish tint of his skin in the lantern light. And he smelled awful. Still, money was money. Luke and I hauled the corpse to the wagon while Chester started filling in the grave. We laid Monsieur Moreau in back and then helped Chester smooth down the dirt by the headstone. I tossed the canvas on top of Monsieur Moreau's body to conceal it as we got back into the wagon.

Our second snatch had been buried in a cemetery a little to the east of town. We headed out that way in high spirits. We were going to make a fortune!

The only light along the tree-lined avenue came from Luke's lantern. It made strange flickering shadows on the underside of the branches. You don't realize how noisy the night is—what with the buzz of chirping insects, the rustle of night creatures roaming the bushes, and the calling of night birds—until all that sound ceases abruptly, as it had now. And from somewhere in back of the wagon, a moaning sound began: Oooo. Ooooo!

RESURRECTIONISTS

The sound started low but grew in volume and rose in pitch until it echoed up and down the shadowy lane and the whole wagon shook with it. My ears hurt and my teeth buzzed unpleasantly, but that was nothing compared to the shudders of fear shaking my body and the chills crawling all over my skin.

"Cut it out, Luke. That isn't funny," Chester shouted as the horses nervously swerved first to one side of the road and then to the other, their ears pricked backward in anxiety. His hands were shaking on the reins as we broke out of the tree line into a wide meadow with a cow pond on our left.

"It isn't me!" Luke retorted over the escalating sound. He clapped shaking hands over his ears and turned to look back over the seat of the wagon. The dirty tarp was shaking as something struggled to rise from underneath. And then a green light came streaming up through the tarp, shooting over our heads like a bright firework, and started spinning in the air. It rapidly formed into the figure of a skinny old man with a withered face and floppy white hair. He flew right at us, fingers outstretched like claws.

Chester shouted in panic. The horses reared and then plunged off the road, racing down the incline and into the shallow pond. The ghost flew after us; his glowing hands pummeled our faces and pulled at our hair. Every blow was ice cold, as if we were being slapped with winter seawater. Behind us, the moaning sound increased until I thought my eardrums would burst. The horses were chest deep in water and trying desperately to swim, but the wagon stuck fast in the muddy bottom and pulled them to a halt.

I leapt out of the wagon into the pond with a great splash. I waded as fast as I could through muddy water and bulrushes, chased by the irate ghost. As soon as I hit dry land, I ran for my life. The glowing man whirled back toward the wagon and pummeled the escaping Luke and Chester around the ears as they followed me up the slope and down the road. I risked a quick look behind me and saw the moaning corpse of Jacques Moreau rolling in the wagon bed, all tangled up in the tarp. The glowing ghost swooped and tried to free his corpse from the tarp, but his spirit hands were unable to grip it. The horses rolled their eyes in panic but were stuck fast and unable to flee from the frightening vision. I kept running.

Fatigue forced us to a halt, and we lay panting in the center of the dark avenue. We knew we had to go back. We couldn't leave the wagon and the horses in the pond. "And," I said aloud, "we have to rebury the body."

Luke groaned but didn't argue with me. None of us wanted to mess with moaning corpses or savage ghosts for the rest of our lives.

We waited until the shrieks of outrage had ceased before we crept back along the avenue and crouched at the edge of the tree line, looking for the ghost. All was silent in the meadow, and the horses were shifting restlessly in the water as they tried in vain to free themselves from the harness. The body in the wagon bed had ceased moaning and lay still.

Hastily, we pushed and pulled at the wagon until it came unstuck from the pond mud. We guided the trembling horses out of the pond and back up the hill. Then Chester drove at top speed back to the cemetery and we reinterred Jacques Moreau next to the stone put up by his hopeful widow. It was full daylight before we got to Chester's house, and we still had to wash the mud off the wagon before we called it quits for the night.

"Shall we go again tomorrow?" Luke asked half-heartedly when the last bit of mud was removed. Chester and I glared at him. "Or maybe not," he mumbled, backing away hastily. "I'll see you both later." He hastened out of the barn and ran out of the yard, a rumpled figure in water-stained trousers and weedy boots.

"There's got to be a better way to earn money," I said to Chester as I tossed a dirty rag into the rain barrel.

"I'm going to work for the newspaper," Chester said flatly. "And I refuse to cover the obits."

He walked out of the barn without looking back. Ruefully, I watched him go and then headed home myself. If I hurried, I could get cleaned up and still make it down to the docks in time for work. My new boss seemed like an angel from heaven compared to the ghost of Jacques Moreau. I was sure of one thing: My body-snatching days were over!

Resources

All Trails. *Trowbridge Falls Blue Trail Loop.* San Francisco, CA: Alltrails.com. https://www.alltrails.com/trail/canada/ontario/trowbridge-falls-blue-trail-loop

Asfar, Dan. *Ghost Stories of Michigan.* Edmonton, AB: Ghost House Publishing, 2002.

———. *Ghost Stories of Pennsylvania.* Edmonton, AB: Ghost House Books, 2002.

Asfar, Dan, and Edrick Thay. *Ghost Stories of America.* Edmonton, AB: Ghost House Books, 2001.

Barber, Sally. *Myths and Mysteries of Michigan.* Guilford, CT: Globe Pequot Press, 2012.

Battle, Kemp P. *Great American Folklore.* New York: Doubleday & Company, Inc., 1986.

Berketa, Rick. *Niagara Falls: The Maid of the Mist, a History.* https://www.niagarafrontier.com/maidmist.html (accessed August 1, 2004).

Bielski, Ursula. *Haunts of the White City.* Charleston, SC: Haunted America, 2019.

Bierce, Ambrose. *Present at a Hanging and Other Ghost Stories.* Urbana, IL: Project Gutenberg, 1913. https://www.gutenberg.org/ebooks.

Bishop, Hugh E. *Haunted Lake Superior.* Duluth, MN: Lake Superior Port Cities Inc., 2003.

Botkin, B. A., ed. *A Treasury of American Folklore.* New York: Crown, 1944.

Boyer, Dennis. *Driftless Spirits.* Madison, WI: Prairie Oak Press, 1996.

———. *Giants in the Land: Folk Tales and Legends of Wisconsin.* Madison, WI: Prairie Oak Press, 2000.

———. *Northern Frights!* Oregon, WI: Badger Books Inc., 1998.

Boyers, Dwight. *Ghost Ships of the Great Lakes.* Cleveland, OH: Freshwater Press, Inc., 1968.

Brewer, J. Mason. *American Negro Folklore.* Chicago: Quadrangle Books, 1972.

Brown, Charles E. *Brimstone Bill.* Madison: Wisconsin Historical Society, 1942. Online facsimile at www.wisconsinhistory.org/turningpoints/search.asp?id=1622; accessed May 1, 2007.

———. *Ghost Tales.* Madison: Wisconsin Historical Society, 1931. Online facsimile at www.wisconsinhistory.org/turningpoints/search.asp?id=1622; accessed May 1, 2007.

———. *Johnny Inkslinger.* Madison: Wisconsin Historical Society, 1944. Online facsimile at www.wisconsinhistory.org/turningpoints/search.asp?id=1622; accessed May 1, 2007.

———. *Paul Bunyan Tales.* Madison: Wisconsin Historical Society, 1922. Online facsimile at www.wisconsinhistory.org/turningpoints/search.asp?id=1622; accessed May 1, 2007.

———. *Whiskey Jack Yarns.* Madison: Wisconsin Historical Society, 1940. Online facsimile at www.wisconsinhistory.org/turningpoints/search.asp?id=1622; accessed May 1, 2007.

Brunvand, Jan Harold. *The Choking Doberman and Other Urban Legends.* New York: W. W. Norton, 1984.

———. *The Vanishing Hitchhiker.* New York: W. W. Norton, 1981.

Charles, Veronika Martenova. *Maiden of the Mist.* New York: Stoddard Publishing Company Limited, 2001.

Christensen, Jo-Anne. *Ghost Stories of Illinois.* Auburn, WA: Lone Pine Publishing, 2000.

Coffin, Tristram P., and Hennig Cohen, eds. *Folklore from the Working Folk of America.* New York: Doubleday, 1973.

———. *Folklore in America.* New York: Doubleday & AMP, 1966.

Cohen, Daniel. *Ghostly Tales of Love and Revenge.* New York: Andrew Publishing Group, 1992.

Cohen, Daniel, and Susan Cohen. *Hauntings and Horrors.* New York: Dutton Children's Books, 2002.

Colombo, John Robert. *Ghost Stories of Canada*. Toronto, Ontario: Hounslow Press, 2000.

———. *Mysteries of Ontario*. Toronto, Ontario: Hounslow Press, 1999.

"Death or Insanity. The Fate of Searchers for a Mysterious Buried Treasure." *Duluth Daily Tribune* (Minnesota), April 17, 1890.

Dewhurst, C. Kurt, and Yvonne R. Lockwood, eds. *Michigan Folklife Reader*. East Lansing: Michigan State University Press, 1988.

Donaldson, Karen Hoisington. *Haunted Houses of Michigan*. Self-published, 1988.

Dorson, R. M. *America in Legend*. New York: Pantheon Books, 1973.

———. *Bloodstoppers and Bearwalkers*. Cambridge, MA: Harvard University Press, 1952.

Dziama, Doug, and Jennifer Teed Dziama. *Ghosts of the North Coast: Legends, Mysteries and Haunted Places of Northern Ohio*. Gettysburg, PA: Second Chance, 2013.

Erdoes, Richard, and Alfonso Ortiz. *American Indian Myths and Legends*. New York: Pantheon Books, 1984.

Fowke, Edith. *Folklore of Canada*. Toronto: McClelland & Stewart Limited, 1976.

———. *Legends Told in Canada*. Toronto: Royal Ontario Museum, 1994.

Franklin, Dixie. *Haunts of the Upper Great Lakes*. Holt, MI: Thunder Bay Press, 1997.

Freygood, Steven. *Headless George and Other Tales Told in Canada*. Toronto: Key Porter Books, 1983.

"From the Sandusky Ohio Register. A First Rate Ghost Story." *Providence (RI) Evening Press*, April 9, 1860.

Gethard, Chris. *Weird New York*. New York: Sterling Publishing Co., Inc., 2005.

Godfrey, Linda S. *Haunted Wisconsin: Ghosts and Strange Phenomena of the Badger State, 2nd ed.* Guilford, CT: Globe Pequot Press, 2021.

———. *Monsters of Wisconsin*. Mechanicsburg, PA: Stackpole Books, 2011.

————. *Weird Michigan*. New York: Sterling Publishing Co., Inc., 2006.

Godfrey, Linda S., and Richard D. Hendricks. *Weird Wisconsin*. New York: Sterling Publishing Co., Inc., 2005.

Great Runs. *Trowbridge Falls & Centennial Park*. https://greatruns .com/thunder-bay-on-trowbridge-falls-and-centennial-park

Greenough, William Parker. *Canadian Folk-Life and Folk-Lore*. Amsterdam: Fredonia Books, 2002.

Gurvis, Sandra. *Myths and Mysteries of Ohio: True Stories of the Unsolved and Unexplained*. Guilford, CT: Globe Pequot Press, 2014.

Hammond, Amberrose. *Ghosts and Legends of Michigan's West Coast*. Charleston, SC: Haunted America, 2009.

Hauck, Dennis William. *Haunted Places: The National Directory*. New York: Penguin Books, 2002.

"Haunted Homes Not Shunned Everywhere." *Duluth News Tribune* (Minnesota), August 1, 1915.

"A Haunted House. The Wild, Weird Antics of an Animated Skeleton." *Cleveland Plain Dealer*, March 10, 1889.

"Haunted Houses." *Duluth News Tribune* (Minnesota), July 4, 1920.

Hervy, Sheila. *Canada Ghost to Ghost*. Toronto: Stoddart Publishing Co. Limited, 1996.

————. *Some Canadian Ghosts*. Markham, ON: Simon & Schuster of Canada, 1973.

Hivert-Carthew, Annick. *Ghostly Lights*. Chelsea, MI: Wilderness Adventure Books, 1998.

Hunter, Gerald S. *Haunted Michigan*. Chicago: Lake Claremont Press, 2000.

————. *More Haunted Michigan*. Chicago: Lake Claremont Press, 2003.

Jarvis, Dale. *Haunted Shores*. St. John's, Newfoundland: Flanker Press, Ltd., 2004.

Jones, Louis C. *Things That Go Bump in the Night*. New York: Hill and Wang, 1959.

Kachuba, John B. *Ghosthunting Ohio*. Covington, KY: Clerisy Press, 2004.

Katz, Michael Jay. *Buckeye Legends: Folktales and Lore from Ohio*. Ann Arbor: University of Michigan Press, 1994.

Ketonen, Kris. *Haunted Thunder Bay. Myths, Legends, and Strange Encounters*. Thunder Bay, ON: The Walleye.ca. http://www.thewalleye.ca/haunted-thunder-bay

———. *Thunder Bay's Lucky Paranormal Shares Some Halloween Ghost-hunting Tips*. Ontario, CA: CBC, 2022. https://www.cbc.ca/news/canada/thunder-bay/thunder-bay-haunted-1.6631499

Krejci, William G. *Haunted Put-in-Bay*. Charleston, SC: Haunted America, 2017.

Kuclo, Marion. *Michigan Haunts and Hauntings*. Lansing, MI: Thunder Bay Press, 1992.

Leach, M. *The Rainbow Book of American Folk Tales and Legends*. New York: World Publishing Co., 1958.

Leary, James P. *Wisconsin Folklore*. Madison: University of Wisconsin Press, 1998.

Leeming, David, and Jake Page. *Myths, Legends, and Folktales of America*. New York: Oxford University Press, 1999.

Levy, Hannah Heidi, and Brian G. Borton. *Famous Wisconsin Ghosts and Ghost Hunters*. Oregon, WI: Badger Books Inc., 2005.

Lewis, Chad, and Terry Fisk. *The Michigan Road Guide to Haunted Locations*. Eau Claire, WI: Unexplained Research Publishing Company, 2013.

———. *The Wisconsin Road Guide to Haunted Locations*. Eau Claire, WI: Unexplained Research Publishing Company, 2004.

Long, Megan. *Ghosts of the Great Lakes*. Toronto: Lynx Images, Inc., 2003.

Lyons, Sandy Arno. *Michigan's Most Haunted: A Ghostly Guide to the Great Lakes State*. Troy, MI: SkateRight Publishing, 2007.

Macken, Lynda Lee. *Empire Ghosts*. Forked River, NJ: Black Cat Press, 2004.

Mahieu, Devon. *Haunted Northern Michigan: Presque Isle Lighthouse.* Traverse City, MI: UpNorthLive.com, 2019. https://upnorthlive .com/news/local/haunted-northern-michigan-presque-isle -lighthouse

Manguel, Alberto, ed. *The Oxford Book of Canadian Ghost Stories.* Toronto: Oxford University Press, 1990.

Marchiewskie, Kathie. "Mysterious Light." *The Bay City Times* (Michigan), October 27, 2000.

Marimen, Mark. *Haunted Indiana.* Holt, MI: Thunder Bay Press, 1997.

Marimen, Mark, James A. Willis, and Troy Taylor. *Weird Indiana.* New York: Sterling Publishing Co., Inc., 2008.

"A Maritime Ghost." *Cincinnati Daily Enquirer*, September 12, 1869.

Matson, Elizabeth, and Stuart Stotts. *The Bookcase Ghost.* Shorewood, WI: Midwest Traditions, 1996.

Mayo, William & Mayo, Kathryn. *The Mysterious North Shore of Lake Superior: A Collection of Short Stories About Ghosts, UFOs, Shipwrecks, and More.* Cambridge, MN: Adventure Publications, 2022.

McSherry, Frank D., Jr., Charles G. Waugh, and Martin H. Greenberg, eds. *Ghosts of the Heartland.* Nashville, TN: Rutledge Hill Press, 1990.

Morris, Jeff, and Vince Shields. *Chicago Haunted Handbook: 99 Ghostly Places You Can Visit in and Around the Windy City.* Covington, KY: Clerisy Press, 2013.

Mott, A. S. *Ghost Stories of America, Volume II.* Edmonton, AB: Ghost House Books, 2003.

———. *Ghost Stories of Wisconsin.* Auburn, WI: Lone Pine Publishing International, 2006.

"Mystery Surrounds Deserted House; Haunted, Some Say." *Duluth News Tribune* (Minnesota), November 1, 1909.

Norman, Michael. *Haunted Wisconsin*, 3rd ed. Madison, WI: Terrace Books, 2011.

Norman, Michael, and Beth Scott. *Historic Haunted America.* New York: Tor Books, 1995.

Oleszewski, Wes. *Ghost Ships, Gales, & Forgotten Tales: True Adventures on the Great Lakes.* Gwinn, MI: Avery Color Studios, 1995.

―――. *True Tales of Ghosts & Gales.* Gwinn, MI: Avery Color Studios, 2003.

Otto, Simon. *Walk in Peace: Legends and Stories of the Michigan Indians.* Grand Rapids, MI: Michigan Indian Press, 1990.

Pattskyn, Helen. *Ghosthunting Michigan.* Covington, KY: Clerisy Press, 2012.

Peck, Catherine, ed. *A Treasury of North American Folk Tales.* New York: W. W. Norton, 1998.

Pitkin, David J. *Ghosts of the Northeast.* New York: Aurora Publications, 2002.

"Place Haunted." *Duluth News Tribune* (Minnesota), July 12, 1899.

Pohlen, Jerome. *Oddball Wisconsin.* Chicago: Chicago Review Press, 2001.

Polley, J., ed. *American Folklore and Legend.* New York: Reader's Digest Association, 1978.

Postovit, Mike. *Spooky Kingston: Skeleton Park, the final resting place for thousands.* Global News.ca, 2019. https://globalnews.ca/news/6104744/kingstons-skeleton-park-resting-place-thousands.

"Pot of Gold, Buried Years Ago, is Found. Children of Minnesota Miser Find Fortune Hidden." *Grand Forks Daily Herald* (North Dakota), February 20, 1907.

Presque Isle Township Museum Society. *Old Presque Isle Lighthouse (1840).* Presque Isle, MI: Presqueislelighthouses.org, 2024. https://www.presqueislelighthouses.org/lighthouses/old-presque-isle-lighthouse-1840

Quackenbush, Jannette. *Ohio Ghost Hunter Guide II: Haunted Hocking: A Ghost Hunter's Guide II to Ohio.* Columbus, OH: 21 Crows Dusk to Dawn Publishing, 2013.

Rath, Jay. *The W-Files: True Reports of Wisconsin's Unexplained Phenomena.* Black Earth, WI: Trails Books, 1997.

Reevy, Tony. Ghost Train! Lynchburg, Va.: TLC Publishing, 1998.

Renner, James. *It Came From Ohio . . .: True Tales of the Weird, Wild, and Unexplained*. Cleveland, OH: Gray, 2012.

Revai, Cheri. *The Big Book of New York Ghost Stories*. Mechanicsburg, PA: Stackpole Books, 2000.

———. *Haunted New York*. Mechanicsburg, PA: Stackpole Books, 2005.

Richards, Beth A., and Chuck L. Gove. *Haunted Cleveland*. Charleston, SC: Haunted America, 2015.

Rider, Geri. *Ghosts of Door County*. Wever, IA: Quixote Press, 1992.

Robinett, Kristy. *Ghosts of Southeast Michigan*. Atglen, PA: Schiffer Publishing Ltd., 2010.

Rule, Leslie. *Coast to Coast Ghosts*. Kansas City, KS: Andrews McMeel Publishing, 2001.

Russell, Lou, and John Russell. *Wisconsin Lore and Legends*. Menomonie, WI: Oak Point Press, 1989.

Schwartz, Alvin. *Scary Stories to Tell in the Dark*. New York: HarperCollins, 1981.

Scott, Beth, and Michael Norman. *Haunted Heartland*. New York: Warner Books, 1985.

———. *Haunted Wisconsin*. Black Earth, WI: Trails Books, 2001.

Sherwood, Roland H. *Maritime Mysteries*. Hantsport, NS: Lancelot Press Limited, 1995.

Skinner, Charles M. *American Myths and Legends, Vol. 1 and 2*. Philadelphia: J. B. Lippincott, 1903.

Smith, Barbara. *Canadian Ghost Stories*. Edmonton, AB: Lone Pine, 2001.

———. *Ontario Ghost Stories*. Edmonton, AB: Lone Pine, 1998.

———. *Ontario Ghost Stories, Volume II*. Edmonton, AB: Lone Pine, 2002.

Smitten, Susan. *Ghost Stories of New York State*. Auburn, WA: Ghost House Books, 2004.

Spence, Lewis. *North American Indians: Myths and Legends Series*. London: Bracken Books, 1985.

"Spooks Seen by Dan Sibbler. Numerous and Varied and No Wonder They Bothered Him. The Ghost in the Locomotive Cab the Most Active. Seeing a Man Freeze Stiff in a Spook Snowstorm." *Cleveland Plain Dealer*, June 18, 1899.

Staggs, S. David. *Ohio Ghost & Monster Handbook*. Scotts Valley, CA: CreateSpace, 2017.

Stampfler, Dianna Higgs. *Michigan's Haunted Lighthouses*. Charleston, SC: The History Press, 2019.

Stansfield, Charles A., Jr. *Haunted Ohio: Ghosts and Strange Phenomena of the Buckeye State*. Mechanicsburg, PA: Stackpole Books, 2008.

Stone, Ted, ed. *13 Canadian Ghost Stories*. Saskatoon, Saskatchewan: Western Producer Prairie Books, 1988.

Stonehouse, Frederick. *Haunted Lake Michigan*. Duluth, MN: Lake Superior Port Cities, Inc., 2006.

———. *Haunted Lakes*. Duluth, MN: Lake Superior Port Cities, Inc., 1997.

———. *Haunted Lakes II*. Duluth, MN: Lake Superior Port Cities, Inc., 2000.

Swetnam, George. *Devils, Ghosts, and Witches: Occult Folklore of the Upper Ohio Valley*. Greensburg, PA: McDonald/Sward, 1988

Teel, Gina. *Ghost Stories of Minnesota*. Edmonton, AB: Ghost House Books, 2001.

Thay, Edrick. Ghost Stories of Indiana. Auburn, WA: Lone Pine Publishing International, 2002.

———. *Ghost Stories of Ohio*. Edmonton, AB: Ghost House Books, 2001.

Trapani, Beth E., and Charles J. Adams III. *Ghost Stories of Pittsburgh and Allegheny County*. Reading, PA: Exeter House Books, 1994.

Tucker, Elizabeth. *Haunted Southern Tier*. Charleston, SC: Haunted America, 2011.

Untermeyer, Louis. *The Wonderful Adventures of Paul Bunyan*. New York: The Heritage Illustrated Bookshelf, 1945.

Veroni, Marshall. *5 Haunted Trails to Explore in Ontario's Deep, Dark Woods*. Ontario: Northern Ontario Travel, 2023.https:// northernontario.travel/outdoor-adventures/haunted-trails-ontario

"Wants Gold Buried by Father." *Duluth News Tribune* (Minnesota), October 11, 1908.

"A Watery Ghost. A Leaky Scow Pumped by a Ghost Which Drags the Captain from His Bunk." *Cincinnati Commercial*, August 30, 1869.

Willis, James A. *The Big Book of Ohio Ghost Stories*. Mechanicsburg, PA: Stackpole Books, 2013.

———. *Ohio's Historic Haunts: Investigating the Paranormal in the Buckeye State*. Kent, OH: Black Squirrel Books, 2015.

Willis, James A., Andrew Henderson, and Loren Coleman. *Weird Ohio*. New York: Sterling, 2005.

Wilson, Patty A. *The Pennsylvania Ghost Guide*, Vol. 1. Waterfall, PA: Piney Creek Press, 2000.

———. *The Pennsylvania Ghost Guide*, Vol. 2. Waterfall, PA: Piney Creek Press, 2001.

Wincik, Stephanie. Ghosts of Erie County. Self-published, 2002.

Winfield, Mason. *Shadows of the Western Door*. Buffalo, NY: Western New York Wares, Inc., 1997.

———. *Spirits of the Great Hill*. Buffalo, NY: Western New York Wares, Inc., 2001.

———. *Haunted Places of Western New York*. Buffalo, NY: Western New York Wares, Inc., 2006.

Woodyard, Chris. *Ghost Hunter's Guide to Haunted Ohio*. Dayton, OH: Kestrel Publications, 2000.

———. *Haunted Ohio: Ghostly Tales from the Buckeye State*. Beaver Creek, OH: Kestrel Publications, 1991.

Wyman, Walker D. *Wisconsin Folklore*. River Falls: University of Wisconsin, 1979.

Zeitlin, Steven J., Amy J. Kotkin, and Holly Cutting Baker. *A Celebration of American Family Folklore*. New York: Pantheon Books, 1982.

About the Author

S. E. Schlosser has been telling stories since she was a child, when games of "let's pretend" quickly built themselves into full-length tales acted out with friends. A graduate of Houghton College, the Institute of Children's Literature, and Rutgers University, she created  and maintains the award-winning website AmericanFolklore. net, where she shares a wealth of stories from all fifty states, some dating back to the origins of America. Sandy spends much of her time answering questions from visitors to the site. Many of her favorite emails come from other folklorists who delight in practicing the old tradition of who can tell the tallest tale.

About the Illustrator

Artist **Paul G. Hoffman** trained in painting and printmaking, and his first extensive illustration work was on assignment in Egypt, drawing ancient wall reliefs for the University of Chicago. His work graces books of many genres—children's titles, textbooks, short story collections, natural history volumes, and numerous cookbooks. For *Spooky Great Lakes* he employed a scratchboard technique and an active imagination.